Listening to Children Reading

UKRA Teaching of Reading Monographs

Advisory editors 1977–
Asher Cashdan, Head of Department of Communication Studies
Sheffield City Poltytechnic
Alastair Hendry, Principal Lecturer in Primary Education
Craigie College of Education

Listening to Children Reading
Helen Arnold

Advisory editor to the series (1971–7)
John E. Merritt, Professor of Educational Studies,
The Open University, Milton Keynes

Reading Readiness
John Downing and Derek Thackray

Reading, Writing and Relevance
Mary Hoffman

Modern Innovations in the Teaching of Reading
Donald Moyle and Louise M. Moyle

Reading: Tests and Assessment Techniques
(new edition in preparation)
Peter D. Pumfrey

Reading and the Consumer
Alma Williams

Print and Prejudice
Sarah Goodman Zimet (with an additional chapter by Mary Hoffman)

Listening to Children Reading

Helen Arnold

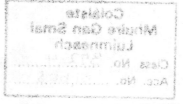

Hodder and Stoughton
In association with the United Kingdom Reading Association

British Library Cataloguing in Publication Data

Arnold, Helen
   Listening to children reading – (UKRA teaching of reading monographs).
   1. Reading (Elementary).   2. Oral reading.
   I. Title   II. Series
   372.4   LB1573.5

   ISBN 0-340-26298-2

Photoset by Rowland Phototypesetting Ltd
Bury St Edmunds, Suffolk
Printed and bound for
Hodder and Stoughton Educational,
a division of Hodder and Stoughton Ltd,
Mill Road, Dunton Green, Sevenoaks, Kent,
by St Edmundsbury Press,
Bury St Edmunds, Suffolk.

Contents

Acknowledgments

I owe thanks to many people for their inspiration and help in the production of this book: among others, to Vera Southgate Booth and the Schools Council, since without the valuable experience of working as a research associate on the 'Extending Beginning Reading' project, I might never have become fascinated by children's oral reading; to Asher Cashdan, for his encouragement and precise criticism; to Mrs Mapperly, the Head of Stoke-by-Clare County Primary School, Suffolk, and her eager readers; to Mrs Mavis Hilton, Primary Adviser, Suffolk County Council, and to the many teachers across the country who have discussed the problems of listening to children reading with me and have helped me to work out a practical method of miscue analysis.

Helen Arnold

Introduction

Learning to read is a matter of intense concern to children, parents and teachers. For children and their parents it is probably one of the earliest and most obvious signs of intellectual achievement; teachers often see it as a mark of their own success or failure, and courses on reading are therefore always heavily over-subscribed. In spite of the enormous amount of reading research that has been published in the last twenty years – perhaps because of it – it is recognised that the reading process is highly complex, and no one method of teaching reading has been found to ensure universal success. As in most educational fields, fashions come and go, with the main conflict over reading being between exponents of a 'Phonic' or a 'Look-and-say' approach; a fruitless argument, since most teachers know that a mixture of methods is preferable. The Bullock Report (*A Language for Life*), published seven years ago, made firm statements about the 'universal truths' of reading acquisition. Learning to read cannot be disassociated from the child's use of spoken language; he learns to read, as he learns everything else, through active participation.

> Let us, therefore, express our conclusion at the outset in plain terms: there is no one method, medium, approach, device or philosophy that holds the key to the process of learning to read [Bullock, 6.1].

The Report gives a clear and detailed account of the reading process, indicating the levels of language in use. Unfortunately, as soon as a process is analysed it must be written about sequentially, so that it begins to look like a check-list of discrete skills which can be taught separately and in order. It is possibly more important than getting bogged down in the technical details to appreciate the philosophy behind Bullock. For example,

> All genuine learning involves discovery, and it is as ridiculous to suppose that teaching begins and ends with 'instruction' as it is to suppose that 'learning by discovery' means leaving children to their own resources [Bullock, 4.10].

For teachers of large and lively classes, the constraints of numbers must affect methods of instruction. A pattern of teaching evolves which is accepted as 'conventional wisdom' by the vast majority because it seems to work best in given circumstances. The almost universal use of reading schemes emphasises the extrinsically motivated aspect of reading, with everyone concerned sharing in the drive to help the learner to 'crack the code' as quickly as possible. There is little time to stand back, observing and evaluating what learning to read really means to children. There is no doubt that we are successful in producing 'code-crackers'. What we seem less able to develop are children who read independently and critically and who will go on doing so throughout their lives. One reason for this may be the attitudes formed towards the skill at an early age.

This book looks at one aspect of teaching reading which has developed alongside the use of the reading scheme—the practice of hearing children read aloud. The teacher is invited to stand back and think about the good, and less good, facets of that practice. It suggests ways in which more time may be spent in encouraging readers to understand what they are doing from the earliest stages. Animals can learn many things: to carry out tasks to order, to develop repeated action patterns which are triggered off by particular signals. No animal, except the human variety, is able to read. Therefore reading must be far more than a stimulus-response mechanism. It is not enough to teach instant verbal response to a graphic display. We do not fully understand the processes of the brain which cause our learning to be different in kind from that of animals, but we do know that human learning is self-generated, encompassing the ability to make conscious choices and to solve problems in different ways.

The first chapter attempts to put the 'reading aloud to teacher' activity into historical perspective. Together with Chapter 2, which analyses the reading process, it examines the strategies used by learners, and questions some of the traditional assumptions which are held about reading instruction. We accept, however, that listening to reading can be a very valuable activity if undertaken with clear purposes.

One of these purposes is covered in Chapter 3; this deals with listening to the child reading *diagnostically*, both formally and informally. The chapter is divided into two broad sections. The first concentrates on what can be gained by observing the deviations from the original text which a child makes in reading aloud (errors or miscues); that is, diagnosis arising from the reading act itself. In the second part we examine a less direct means of diagnosis, in which the teacher learns from discussion with the pupil about his understanding, attitudes and styles of approach to reading. The chapter ends with the suggestion that children themselves can become good evaluators of their own progress.

Chapter 4 illustrates this diagnostic function by presenting case studies of individual children at different stages of reading development, and puts forward a method of analysing miscues which could be of use in the classroom.

In Chapter 5 we move to two other functions of reading aloud. The first follows inevitably from diagnosis, and in practice may proceed jointly with it. This is the *instruction* which the teacher gives, and the ways in which she can encourage the use of all the available cueing systems. The final function leaves the individual teacher/child interaction to suggest ways in which reading aloud to others can be used for *communication*. We believe that, although this does not come naturally to all children, it is a pleasurable and useful skill which will grow best from small-group work.

Chapter 6 tries to solve the difficulties of carrying out these functions in the classroom, and concentrates on organisation. We suggest how reading aloud in all its aspects can be fitted into the overall language curriculum of a class.

The convention has been adopted throughout the text of referring to the teacher as 'she' and the pupil as 'he' in order to avoid ambiguity.

1   The existing practice, and its origins

A muted buzz is heard as the classroom door opens; children sit in groups at tables dotted round the bright and picture-packed room. Some heads are bent over maths books, while other children are writing stories and diaries. The teacher sits at her desk with an open register and calls a child's name, who proceeds to her table armed with a book and takes up position by the teacher's shoulder. The 'reading book', one of several different schemes displayed on bookshelves and tables, is placed on the teacher's desk and opened at the page indicated on a small card placed within the book. The child begins to read aloud, while the teacher listens, one eye and ear cocked towards the reader, and the other monitoring the varied activities of the class. After about thirty seconds there is an interruption. Another child approaches waving his 'word-book' and asks for a spelling. The reader continues stolidly. Three minutes and five interruptions later the teacher stops him, marks the page reached on his card, ticks his name on her register and dismisses him kindly if rather absent-mindedly, her glance already on the next name on the register. The child returns to his table and continues to read *sotto voce* until his attention is distracted by a friend asking to borrow a rubber.

It is superfluous to describe this scene to most primary teachers, since it has become the accepted background organisation to reading instruction in innumerable classrooms throughout the country, rooted in origins whose history has never been traced. 'Hearing children read' provides the core of reading teaching, and reading schemes the content. Whole word recognition of words on flash cards, phonic drills, and exercises in comprehension are taught to whole classes, or, less often, to small groups, but the daily individual contact with any one child is made through the 'reading aloud' interaction. Very little direct instruction is given during the interview, nor is the content of the reading matter often discussed. The aim, for both teacher and child, is to record as rapid progress as possible through the reading scheme. Learning appears to be achieved incidentally because the scheme is graded carefully for readability. New words are learnt through the extensive repetition which occurs. Progress may be very slow or meteoric. Whatever else, it is certain that every child knows where he is in the reading pecking order, since each book in the scheme is clearly numbered and often distinguished by different colours, and the encouragement of oral reading makes the activity public and competitive.

Since the 'hearing of reading' is so popular it is important to pinpoint the attitudes and philosophies underlying the practice, and to attempt to place it in an historical background.

Teachers, parents and children alike probably see reading as the most overt sign of language achievement. Although it is recognised that reading is only one of the language modes, and that children who come from 'linguistically deprived' backgrounds may find it harder to learn to read, the impetus is towards early mastery rather than the building up of confidence in talking and listening skills. The belief that learning to read should await the moment of 'readiness' has been discredited to some extent in the eyes of teachers, who find that most children in a literate society are geared towards the printed words surrounding them, on television screens and shop signs, if not in books, long before they come to school. *Breakthrough to Literacy* (Mackay *et al.*, 1970), the result of a Schools' Council project, seemed to have a considerable influence on methods of teaching beginning reading, accentuating as it did the importance of children learning to say, read, and write simultaneously the words they needed. Their reading primers were supplementary to the central aims of sentence and word makers, and therefore it appeared possible to break the tradition of the reading scheme. The Primary Survey, *Primary Education in England*, however, published by Her Majesty's Inspectorate (HMSO, 1978), found that *Breakthrough* was only being used in 7 per cent of infant schools. They found that

> The use of graded reading schemes was universal in 7 year old classes . . . by the age of eleven, some children in three-quarters of the classes were making use of reading schemes . . . It was evident that teachers devoted considerable attention to ensuring that children mastered the basic techniques of reading, but there was a tendency at all ages for children to receive insufficient encouragement to extend the range of their reading (op. cit. Section 5.26/5.27).

So teachers have almost universally adopted the graded reading scheme as the main prop for reading instruction, often to quite advanced ages in their pupils. Many middle schools (9–13 years) even, consider a supplementary scheme to be a necessary resource for ensuring systematic progress.

The use of a scheme presupposes that children must be checked frequently in their reading, a sort of inbuilt diagnostic procedure being present because of the careful (or supposedly careful) grading of the scheme. Most teachers believe that regular individual oral reading to an adult is necessary for *all* children up to a third year junior level. If they do not do it, they feel guilty; they will often spend their breaks and dinner-hours 'catching up' with the children they have missed. The report *Nine Hundred Primary School Teachers* (Bassey, 1978) found that both infant and junior teachers heard children read aloud frequently – of 281 infants teachers questioned, an average of 78 per cent expected to hear *all* children read aloud three times a week *at least*. 34 per cent heard their children read every day. In junior classes (aged 7–11) 64 per cent believed that all children should read aloud regularly to the teacher or an adult. The reading was predominately from a structured reading scheme.

Most of the assessment of reading development, therefore, comes from listening to oral reading, and rests largely on word-recognition facility. From the occasional administration of a standardised word-recognition test (most popularly Schonell or Burt) to the card in the reader which may note the words which have caused difficulty, achievement means being able to decode 'fluently'. The belief in the efficacy of this approach is now solidly backed by the expectations of all involved. Headmasters often check that teachers are hearing children read frequently, the children feel neglected if they are not called to the teacher's desk as often as others, and parents take it as the main evidence of the teacher's personal interest in their children.

It is possible to summarise the underlying beliefs which support this practice, even though they are rarely articulated. The first is a belief in evaluating the *achievement* of the skill rather than analysis of the different processes which contribute to the very complicated mastery of reading. The second is the importance placed on quantity rather than quality, the drive to 'get through the scheme' as quickly as possible. The most successful are the readers who climb this vertical ladder rather than learning how to enjoy and use reading at whatever level of development they have reached. The third belief (often unconsciously held), is that 'learning to read' is different from other aspects of cognitive learning; it is the skill of decoding, ideally as automatised as possible, which is equated with learning to ride a bicycle or climbing ropes in PE. The understanding of reading is a different faculty, to be mastered by the frequent use of comprehension exercises. Many reading schemes list at the back the new items of vocabulary which have been included in a particular book. Sometimes the teacher will save time by checking that these 'new' words have been mastered rather than hearing the story read. It is quantity of vocabulary assimilation which appears to be important rather than an interest in the growth of conceptual frameworks. Reading matter which occurs in other subject areas (for example, mathematics) is not used to teach reading; this often results in a strange mismatch between the fairly simple basis and structure of the scheme and the sophisticated terminology of modern maths books. It usually means that the teacher reads and explains the text of the maths problem to the child rather than encouraging functional reading for a purpose.

There is often also a lack of direct connection between the teacher reading stories to the children and the 'learning-to-read' process. The enjoyment in narrative, the excitement of the shared experience, are all too often confined to 'story-time', while the child thinks that his reading book is solely for 'learning new words' or 'learning how to spell better'. A child who was able to read, with natural intonation, at a normal rate, many books at home, took a copy of the reading scheme home to his mother and chanted it out word-by-word to her. When asked why he was reading in such a 'funny' way, he replied that that was how you were supposed to read your book at school. 'Everybody does it like that.'

The Schools' Council *Extending Beginning Reading* Project (Southgate *et al.*, 1981) asked teachers in the first two years of junior school to state their objectives in teaching reading and allied skills. Increase of proficiency in the basic skill was mentioned by nearly every teacher, which was often related directly to achievement in word-recognition and word-attack. 'Fluency' was often cited as a separate component from 'comprehension', implying that fluency was seen as efficient oral reading. As pupils got older, teachers tended to spend more time on hearing backward readers, while those who had reached a satisfactory level in reading aloud were more often engaged in writing activities; the time they spent on silent reading was not noticeably increased.

Twenty-three teachers kept open-ended logsheets to include anything that they considered as 'reading activities', over a period of ten weeks. The information yielded by the logs showed that the predominant activity was listening to children reading. Most teachers were involved in this for anything between 20 and 40 minutes, occasionally 60–100 minutes daily, in both first and second year junior classes. Only two teachers claimed never to listen to their above average readers. Half thought that they listened to below average readers daily, and the remainder considered 2–3 times a week appropriate. Average readers were heard 2–3 times a week. The same allocation seemed to operate regardless of the stage of development of the reader.

The logs indicated that a reading session with one child might last from 1 to 15 minutes, with an average of 2–3 minutes per child. A small percentage of teachers used both individual and group organisation, but the great majority dealt with children individually. The books used for hearing reading were invariably teacher-selected 'reading books', usually from a scheme, with *Wide Range Readers* heading the list and *Through the Rainbow* taking second place.

The teachers' logs were backed by observations made by the re-searchers, of both teacher and child behaviour in any lesson which might include reading and/or writing. The category 'Teacher hears oral reading' took up 14 per cent of the teacher's time on average in both years, contrasting with, for example, 4 per cent of her time being spent in giving direct reading instruction and 4 per cent of the time in expanding on or explaining the content of text. It emerged from the observations that the time spent on hearing reading with any one child was constantly inter-rupted by other pupils needing help. 'The average time spent by a teacher in total concentration on a child's oral reading was only thirty seconds.' So, whereas in the logs teachers indicated that they thought they were devoting up to fifteen minutes to a child, in practice this was chopped up into tiny segments of time. Only rarely did a teacher ask any questions, even at a literal level, on book content; the practice was specifically 'hearing' a child read, with prompting of single words where necessary.

As far as observation of individual children was concerned, the contact with the teacher was inevitably infrequent, since classes were usually around the thirty mark. In the first year of junior school, 5.8 per cent of a child's time on average was spent in reading his assigned book, rising to 11.5 per cent in the second year (the figure including silent reading as well as reading to the teacher). An average of 33.3 per cent of all children's time was spent in 'non-oriented' activity, some of which was accounted for by waiting for the teacher's help or instruction.

The researchers on the project found it difficult to draw any statistically significant conclusions on causal relationships between achievement on pre-test and post-test standardised reading scores and teaching style, due to the great number of variables operating in any classroom. However, there was a suggestion (Chapter 15) of a correlation between the time teachers spent on listening to reading and the reading progress of the class. Two classes which achieved on average more highly on the post-tests (Brimer *Wide-Span* and *Southgate Group Reading Tests*) were those whose teachers placed *least* emphasis on reading aloud to the teacher. Maxwell (1977, p. 32) found likewise that 'there was no relationship between regular oral reading by individual pupils and class attainment and progress in reading' over the first three years in primary school classes in Scotland.

It appears that the vast majority of teachers in the early years of schooling believe that in hearing children read they are carrying out the individualised teaching which is expected of them. Since most children eventually succeed in learning to read with a variety of organisations and method-ological approaches, little evidence has been put forward to question the efficiency of the present practice.

Children operate within and support the practice and quickly develop attitudes and expectations which tend to perpetuate it. They, too, hold certain, usually unexpressed, beliefs about learning to read. The first is the necessity to know where they are in relation to others, so that they can measure their own progress, since early reading is usually extrinsically motivated. Progression through the reading scheme or schemes is admirably geared to allow them this knowledge.

They believe also that reading is a skill to be mastered once and for all. An eight-year-old boy in the Extending Beginning Reading project was asked 'Do you think you ought to learn to read?' Having answered in the affirmative, he was then asked, 'Why do you think you should?', to which the reply was 'Then I can stop', a response which might have been thought of, even though not expressed, by many less honest pupils!

Children believe that getting behind on the scheme indicates failure, and are therefore likely to feel inferior to their peers when this occurs. Since 'reading to teacher' is closely linked in their minds with ticking off the pages read, they probably think that the more times they are heard read, the quicker they will progress. (Logistically this is likely to be so in many cases, as they do not read much on their own from the book in between sessions.) However, one of the reasons given by teachers for hearing children read frequently – that the children like it – was refuted by two-thirds of the sample of 7–9 year olds in the Extending Beginning Reading project, who said that they preferred reading quietly to themselves rather than out loud to the teacher. Six children in the second year thought that silent reading was quicker than reading aloud, with one boy expanding 'You don't have to stop to breathe. I lose myself in it . . . I work myself into the book' (Southgate *et al.*, op cit).

Parents are likely to expect their children to learn to read as soon as possible on school entry, and accept that the amount of time the teacher spends listening to their children is commensurate with the amount of instruction they are receiving. They may view reading as predominately a decoding skill; schools have in the past adopted the *Ladybird* scheme in self-defence, as it is the only one freely available for general purchase; parents are therefore likely to buy it and insist on their children reading to them every night. The Belfield Experiment, reported in the *Sunday Times* in March 1981, showed how parents were encouraged to carry some of the onus of helping children in cooperation with the teacher. This could be one way in which the amount of hearing reading in school could be reduced. 'Every night, the Belfield children each take home a reading book and a card. The child reads for 10 or 15 minutes to a parent, who then initials the card and makes comments on the child's progress'. Next day, the teacher discusses what has been read with the child.

The Bullock Report (Bullock, 1975) stated that 'most teachers, in striving for fluency, set a premium on a quick, confident and unhesitating delivery of the words' (17.18). Certainly it seems that attitudes of teachers, parents and children tend to support oral reading practice, often prolonged for some years, thereby probably keeping the child on 'word-by-word' reading, with a consequent delay in extended silent reading, which is harder to check and impossible to itemise on a progress chart. Since the practice of hearing reading is universal, an attempt will now be made to trace its origins, and to find how firm the foundation is upon which it has been built.

TRACING THE ROOTS OF THE TRADITION

Historical influences

The teaching of reading in the early stages of compulsory education in England was guided by the notion that constant repetition would ensure mastery; the mastery, though, was of a very limited skill. To gain her 'Payment by Results' a teacher needed only to prepare her pupils to read aloud some single words and a paragraph or so of continuous text. The implication at this time was, and remained so for many years, that learning to read was a stimulus–response mechanism. The idea that learners could employ contextual clues in initial reading was only suggested by a few inspired teachers, and psychologists like Huey (1908). Ronald Morris discusses some of these interesting exceptions in *Success and Failure in Learning to Read* (Morris, 1979).

The social impetus behind the drive for universal literacy supported the idea of reading as a strictly functional skill, for improvement rather than enjoyment with firm goals set during the learning. Denis Lawton, quoting R. D. Altick (1975) describes the attitude of what he called 'do-gooders' who wanted to teach the masses to read:

> They deplored what they called the habit of 'desultory reading'. If one were to read at all, it should be with a fixed end in mind. . . . Reading for the sake of reading – finding amusement in one book, instruction in a second, a bit of inspiration in a third – could not be too severely condemned (Lawton, 1975, p. 46).

With this background, it is amazing that the advice given from time to time by the Inspectorate in various publications, should have taken the form it did. They never recommend rote learning, and rarely make mention of children reading aloud individually. On the contrary, they make a good many suggestions which approve quite different methods.

The 1944 HMSO *Handbook of Suggestions for Teachers* says

It is true that at first a great deal of practice in reading aloud will be necessary, especially with less proficient pupils . . . but silent reading for 'content' is equally important; and it should on no account be supposed that reading of this kind is something of which only older children are capable (p. 365).

What was apparently meant by 'reading aloud' in the above report was the prepared delivery of passages to be performed to other children; it aimed at the 'essential quality . . . of clearness of utterance' rather than being a vehicle for the teacher to assess progress. The emphasis was placed so squarely on the communicative function of oral reading that it is suggested that 'the teacher will find herself better able to criticise the reading . . . if she (the teacher) does not always follow it in her own book!' Accurate reproduction of the words of the text was obviously considered either unimportant, or a previously mastered skill not worth mentioning.

In 1950 the Ministry of Education published Pamphlet 18, entitled *Reading Ability – some suggestions for helping the backward.* Their message is clear and worth quoting fully, remembering that they are referring to backward readers rather than high-fliers.

There are some children who will quickly appear to be able to read a passage aloud when in fact they are merely reacting to the symbols of the printed word by making appropriate sounds. It was precisely the point which Matthew Arnold made when complaining bitterly of the effect of 'payment by results' . . . some eighty years ago. A too exclusive use, therefore, of reading aloud has the specific danger that of the three things involved – word pattern, sound and meaning – the last, which is the most important, may go by the board. This draws attention to the value of silent reading. Moreover silent reading techniques allow children more readily to move forward at their own pace (p. 18).

Primary Education (HMSO, 1959) went into rather more detail about methods of teaching the skill, dwelling on the importance of 'getting into reading' through a variety of ways. It criticised the over-use of 'readers', which, due to the fragmentary nature of their content would be unlikely to develop sustained interest. 'Teachers need to contrive times and places so that children can read at length and in peace' (p. 158). Again, there is very little mention of pupils reading aloud to the teacher, but strong support for group reading, except for the very backward.

More recently the Plowden report on *Children and their Primary Schools* (1967) (a title whose order of words is significant), similarly doubted the value of reading schemes.

Reading schemes should never determine the practice adopted for all children. A few children are able, with a little help, to teach themselves to read from books of rhymes and stories learnt by heart. Rather more can pass direct from home-made books to simple story books. Many children will not need to go right through a series of books: others will require a great deal of supplementary material (Vol. 1, Section 584).

The modernity of these publications is even more surprising when compared with the suggestions in the Bullock Report, *A Language for Life* (HMSO, 1975), which strikes one as more formal and structured than its predecessors in its suggestions for teaching reading. It advises that in order to keep a 'meticulous check' on progress, every child should be heard reading several times a week, with follow-up questions to test comprehension (7.31). In the same paragraph a modifying suggestion is made that small group work can provide valuable shared experience in reading. In the chapter on screening, the Committee report that most teachers used the practice of hearing children as their main means of assessment, considering that administration of standardised tests was the province of the educational psychologist. In answer to questionnaires, 86 per cent of infant teachers and 77 per cent of junior teachers said that they tested a child before he moved on to a new book. The committee concluded that 'it is likely that . . . it took the form of hearing the child read' (17.17). They continue 'but the indications are that its diagnostic possibilities are largely unrealised'. The table below, reproduced from the Bullock Report (p. 252) shows the number of occasions on which 6 and 9 year olds read to their teacher in a week, with the classes of pupils percentaged.

TABLE I

		Daily %	3-4 times weekly %	1-2 times weekly %	Less often %
6 yrs	Ablest readers	17	36	41	6
	Average readers	31	54	15	–
	Poorest readers	72	26	2	–
9 yrs	Ablest readers	1	4	35	59
	Average readers	3	19	64	14
	Poorest readers	48	38	13	1

Reading between the lines of the reports, it seems that individual reading aloud crept into being without direct guidance, but is certainly accepted in the Bullock report to an extent which does not occur in earlier publications.

If not encouraged by advice from 'on high', how was the custom engendered, and why has it become so universal? It seems fanciful to suggest that the influence initially came from the 'Payment by Results' philosophy, so we must perhaps look in other directions to explain its popularity.

Reading schemes and assessment

The earliest reading schemes emphasised the importance of learning the alphabet and its sounds, and of building up words from previously learnt letters. In the thirties and forties new thinking in psychology advocated a more global approach, and it was then that the 'modern' reading scheme was initiated, with illustrations and reading matter designed to interest the young reader in the content of the book. One of the earliest and most popular of such schemes was Schonell's *Happy Venture Readers* (Schonell and Serjeant, 1939), written by a psychologist to support his own theories of child development. The child, if motivated by attractive narrative, with vocabulary carefully selected and graded to enable whole words to be easily recognised and remembered, would learn to read easily himself. The important thing was that the *word* should be the meaningful unit. Since then, emphasis on look-and-say, phonics, diacritical marking systems and so on have fluctuated, but the reading scheme has remained throughout the powerful instrument of whatever methodology was advocated. To an extent, therefore, the teacher became the mediator of the scheme rather than a direct instructor.

Few of the earliest reading experts advocated the practice of individuals reading aloud to a teacher. Schonell himself did not recommend his scheme being used in this way. Rather, he discussed at length other methods of organising instruction, especially the use of small groups (Schonell, 1945a, pp. 67, 84, ff). It probably developed when the teacher realised that certain aspects of the reading skill still had to be taught, to some children at least. Then she began to use the scheme as a direct instructional resource with one child at a time.

Another important element in teaching is the diagnosis and recording of achievement. Schonell and other psychologists in this period became interested in the causes of backwardness in reading. It is hard to tell cause from effect, but the institution of standardised reading tests which posited norms for reading development, defined by a Reading Age, must have made many teachers in classrooms aware for the first time of backwardness as a concept. Expectations would be aroused of what 'should be' in reading attainment. Such expectations led to the provision of handbooks and guides for 'helping the retarded', and eventually to the formation of such bodies as the National Association for Remedial Education.

Nearly all the early tests were of the word-recognition type, designed to be administered to individual children. They were often devised to link with particular methods of teaching reading. For example, Schonell's word-recognition test (Schonell, 1945b), still one of the most widely used, was devised to work in conjunction with *Happy Venture Readers*, a predominantly 'Look-and-Say' scheme. So teachers might begin to use a scheme with individuals, not only for instruction and practice, but to ensure good test results.

Standardised reading tests are often administered by the Headteacher, with the Educational Psychologists and Advisory Teachers giving formal diagnostic tests, like the Neale Analysis (1958), to the few children who seem to be at risk. The teacher herself is unlikely to use a sophisticated form of assessment. Her evaluation of progress will be tied firmly to the progress through the reader. It is at this point that the practice of hearing children read becomes most significant. If she hears an individual read as frequently as possible, his achievement can be checked and recorded, usually on a slip of card which is kept by the child in the book. The teacher's own recording is quantitative rather than qualitative, since it often consists merely of ticking off a name on the register, with an occasional note of words which have presented obstacles during the oral 'read'. Formal assessment of comprehension is rarely made, and it is likely that the pupil will regard the mastery of reading as a speedy march through a series of books, in competition with other readers who may be ahead of or behind him!

Although we have been able to discover little approval for hearing children read from Inspectors or from the authors of reading schemes, it was encouraged from other directions, for instance in books on the teaching of reading aimed to help the teacher of the backward. Often these books were, and are, written by experienced specialists who perhaps have not had to deal so much with large classes as with a few 'remedial' readers. Montessori advocated individual lessons to find each child's abilities, many years ago, but she did suggest that the child should read 'instruction' cards silently, and did not advocate primers. More recently J. Hughes (1975) typifies modern advice by saying, 'The most valuable contribution to the teaching of reading is made when the teacher is in a position to give individual attention to the child ... Ideally, the teacher should listen to children reading every day' (p. 107).

This is put even more forcefully in a recent edition of the valuable *A–Z List of Reading Books*, published by NARE (Atkinson and Gains, 1979). Its introduction, like the Bullock Report, acknowledges the demands made by large classes, but still insists that children should be heard reading frequently. The weekly reading programme designed for a hypothetical second year class suggests eighteen as a reasonable number of individuals to hear daily (p. 11). A footnote states, 'It is rarely possible to hear more than twenty children read orally per day'. If each child were allocated five minutes, a reasonable though not over-generous period for the suggested 'diagnostic' exercise, a total of ninety minutes a day appears necessary to hear children reading 'individually'. It is clear why teachers feel guilty if they are not achieving this target figure.

Child-centred education

Another influence has come from a different source which has helped to confirm the belief that hearing reading is not only advisable, but necessary. This is the philosophy of child-centred education, stemming from Rousseau, Froebel, Montessori and others, confirming the importance of the unique development of every child through natural growth. This philosophy, of course, has much that is good to recommend it, and has had a great positive effect on primary education during the last half-century. It is sometimes difficult for the teacher with a class of thirty children, however, to see how she can carry out the philosophy in practical terms.

Child-centredness meant the discarding of the old methods of teaching reading by chanting and rote-learning in chorus. It was important that the teacher should make individual contact with as many of her pupils as possible during the day. What more sensible than to put two 'needs' together, and use the individual contact time to teach reading? The provision of the graded reader made this eminently practicable, since she could gear each child to his own stage of development by providing the right text. It becomes possible to see how the practice has become so deeply rooted, because it fulfils several different purposes. In practice, in large classes, the time that can be given to each child is usually too short and too interrupted to be beneficial. Many teachers realise this, but feel guilty for questioning what is accepted as necessary. The purpose of this book is to re-examine the practice bearing in mind the constraints of managing large classes, and to decide how it may be used more effectively and purposively.

2 What happens when we read?

It is important that teachers should understand the processes involved in learning to read in order to help pupils to utilise all the available strategies. This is easier said than done, since in spite of the enormous amount of reading research of the past twenty odd years, no universally accepted definitive model has emerged. The research itself has been only indirectly beneficial to classroom teaching, as in the early stages it was mainly concerned with perceptual recognition of words in isolation under experimental conditions, often with adult subjects. Recently, however, there has been much more study of reading in context, which should prove more applicable.

Theories of reading, as with methods of teaching, vary according to the educational climate. There are many reasons why reading research should have become so popular during the sixties and seventies. It may be that Marshall McLuhan (1967), suggesting that print is not the only, nor even the best, conveyor of information, and that it may be a transitory form of communication, provoked believers in reading to analyse how ideas in text are absorbed by the reader. Research into standards of reading achievement (Start and Wells, 1972) suggested that initial reading acquisition did not ensure good reading at a later stage. The Open University's Reading Development Course took the then unusual angle of comparing mature reading processes with those of children learning to read, and so provided a different focus for the many teachers taking the course. Perhaps most important was the influence of psycholinguistics, which saw reading as a cognitive, problem-solving activity rather than a receptive skill. In their own ways, all these influences made the point that reading could not be considered in isolation from other language skills. The right match between reader and text was vital, and this is a much more sophisticated concept than merely selecting a certain level of reading scheme for an individual child.

In this chapter we shall first try to clarify what is meant by 'the text' and 'the reader', and then take the special case of what happens when the reader is a child acquiring the skill. The differences between speaking and writing, and between oral and silent reading, will be discussed so far as they concern classroom practice. The chapter ends with a summary of the particular views of two key figures with regard to 'hearing children read'.

THE TEXT

The text alone, of course, means nothing. Words used in proper combinations are merely a code for the recreation of events and objects and ideas as perceived by the reader. Children in a literate society, who have been exposed to printed notices in streets, on television, on food packets in the home, naturally accept that messages are conveyed by the words they see, and may develop a 'Reading Acquisition Device' analogous with Chomsky's 'Language Acquisition Device' which presupposes a predilection towards the printed word, although this is far from proven. They will not understand, however, the way the written language works as an arbitrary symbol system; the fact that English text has certain features which make it quite different from, for example, the Chinese pictogram. As Goody and Watt (Giglioli, 1972) point out, a phonetic system is much simpler than the thousands of pictograms which can only be remembered by the élite few. Only twenty-six letters have to be learnt, but their possible combinations are infinite.

The important thing for teachers to remember, and to mediate to children as soon as possible (though without of course using the technical terms), is that the patterning of the symbolic system works on three levels, all of which can and should be used from the earliest stages. If the beginning reader is shown how to use his knowledge of context at the same time as recognising symbols, he will from the first make connection between 'cracking the code' and 'getting a message'. The three levels in operation are: (1) the *graphophonological*, which enables the reader to equate a written letter or combination of letters with a sound which he can already make in speech; (2) the *syntactic* level, where the symbols are grouped in certain combinations and sequences, linking with previously absorbed knowledge of word-order and grammar in speech, and (3) the *semantic* level, through which meaning is conveyed, and which can be utilised by linking with previous experience of the content of the text.

Because, in reading, the text is assimilated on all these levels more or less simultaneously, it offers more than one cueing system. Much of written text is redundant because clues are available from more than one level. Redundancy means that information may be duplicated in text; for example we get clues about number from word endings as well as 'content' words, double adjectives may be almost synonymous, and so on. This has great advantages for the reader, but it also has dangers, especially for the teacher trying to assess reading achievement. It is quite possible to read quite 'fluently', but to be using only the graphic and some syntactic cues. The grasp of meaning (the deep structure) cannot be so easily diagnosed.

THE READER

The reader is governed by his perception, and no two readers will ever get exactly the same meaning from what they read. The process they go through, if they are mature readers, however, is likely to be similar. Gibson (Gibson and Levin, 1975) shows well how perception works in relation to reading. Three main functions are in operation; first, the selection of *distinctive features* in the text. When reading two words, for instance – *grave* and *grove* we are aware immediately of the only difference between the words – 'a' as the third letter in the first word and 'o' in the second. We do not need to perceive the rest of the word as carefully. This process leads to 'sampling' of the text, whereby we are guided unconsciously to perceive differences which lead us to grasp the message, using as little effort as possible.

We are helped in this by the facility to perceive *relationships*, of letters within words, of words with each other, and relationships between events in a narrative or account. The desire to see patterns is a human characteristic which is developed in babyhood. The mature reader will see an overall pattern of units in sequence, and the better he is at reading, the bigger the 'chunks' which he will perceive. The expectation that certain patterns will repeat within the symbol system will operate at an unconscious level most of the time, so that response will be automatised (through repetition and practice, as in the achievement of most skills).

The third element of perception which Gibson isolates is *attention*. Attention will be focused on whatever level is needed to make sense of the reading, while the eye skims the text for information. If attention is directed to one level exclusively, for example the graphophonological, the full use of all cueing systems will be inhibited.

Marie Clay examines perceptual activities in *Reading: The Patterning of Complex Behaviour* (Clay, 1972) and sums up thus, 'Reading suggests that the good reader manipulates a network of language, spatial and visual perception cues, and sorts these implicitly but efficiently, searching for dissonant relations and best-fit solutions' (pp. 125–6). One of the most interesting aspects of reading is the 'implicit' nature of part of the response, which leads to the good reader not always reading what is actually on the page, although he does not realise that he is deviating slightly from the actual words. These automatised responses made on an unconscious level make the reading act easy if expectations are high of finding familiar language. It could be that over-emphasis on any one type of cueing, for example, phonic, whole-word recognition, or unfounded guessing, may cause an imbalance in the automatic/active search ratio. It is therefore doubly important that the teacher should observe what strategies are being used rather than following a strictly sequential instructional programme.

CHILDREN LEARNING TO READ

Very few adults can remember exactly how they learnt to read; they may recall the physical characteristics of their books, or the surrounding 'atmosphere' of coercion or encouragement, but not the details of instruction. To help reconstruct what happens in reading acquisition it is enlightening to present a message in an unknown coding system. For example:

⌐∇⌐ ∠∇⊓ ⊖∠ƨ φ∇↓↓.

"⟩△□ƨ ∇~⌐ ∨↓∇⌐, ⊓∇↓↓⌐."

⊓∇↓↓⌐ ∠△↓⌐⊓ ⊖∠ƨ φ∇↓↓.

"○ ⟩∇~ ∨↓∇⌐ φ∇↓↓ ⌐·ʁ↓↓,"

⊓∠ƨ ⊓∇⌐⊓.

There are two approaches to 'decoding' the message. The learner might be presented with 'translations' of each symbol, or he might be encouraged to solve the puzzle with no clues given extraneous to the text. The second approximates more to modern methods of teaching reading, the first to an alphabetic method. It is helpful to try to analyse the cues which can be gained from the passage itself, and the probable order. Discussion with groups of teachers who managed to 'read' the story quite easily without being told what the symbols stood for, established the following points:

Order in which clues are used

1. The use of the *picture*. Visual display is always more arresting than text, but it may be misleading. Is the man holding a ball or a bomb? Is he a man or a boy? (Children, who may have been using pictures to tell their stories for some time, often find it difficult not to rely on them too much.)
2. Looking at commas and full-stops and where words are repeated. Recognition of one or two letters from their position in the word (one-letter words are helpful here).
3. Noticing recurring patterns
   of letters within words, particularly double letters;
   of some letters occurring in other words;
   of words themselves being repeated;
   of word endings repeated (grammatical features).
4. Confirmation of accuracy by checking 'fit' of words in total passage; linking with expectations of what is likely to be there.

So reading is a circular activity; a global over-view, discrimination of distinctive features, final overview. The processes used would probably include scanning, looking for repeated patterns, self-checking. The order or frequency of the strategies used might vary from individual to individual, but the overall pattern would probably be the same:

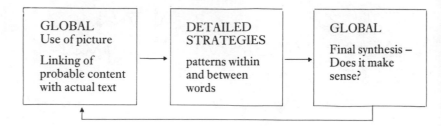

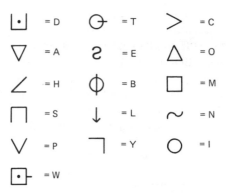

Adults, of course, have an advantage in this simulated exercise over children learning to read, in that they know what letters and words and sentences are, and have a cognitive framework of a symbol system within which to operate. It may well be that one of the most important tasks for a teacher is to help children towards what John Downing calls 'cognitive clarity' (Chapman and Czerniewska, 1978). They may not even realise that the stories that a teacher reads actually come from the book. Downing describes some five-year-olds who thought the stories that were read to them were quite different from the reading in their own books – Mark thought that you get stories 'on the floor – near the piano' (p. 230). Jessie Reid shows, as did Downing later, that there is much confusion among young children over the terms used to describe reading, and that they show more tendency to attach meaning at first not only to pictures but to *numbers*, which have a greater reality for them than letters and words.

It is obvious when one talks to children about their reading, or listens to them employing tactics which they think they ought to be using, rather than those which arise from their own problem-solving tactics, that there is often very great confusion. For instance, 'sounding out' a word with its separate letters – for example t-ă-b-l-ĕ, and then saying 'table' is a quite unreal ploy which cannot have logical reasoning behind it.

The strategies that the learner uses will depend partly, therefore, on his grasp of what reading is all about. The final goal will determine the way he works; if he realises that there is a sensible message to be gleaned he will be looking for meaningful clues. If he thinks that the idea is to 'crack a code' he will be more likely to perceive small units, concentrating on word-recognition. Of course, *all* cues should be used, but the hierarchy of skills will vary.

Psychologists, as we have seen, insist that reading is a problem-solving activity which utilises active search processes, and involves at the same time the use of previous knowledge of written word components which should facilitate a partly automatic response to the print. It is the even balance between these two activities which is difficult to maintain in the child beginner, depending as it does on correct teaching and adequate feedback. While the child is learning to recognise letters and words and to link the graphic symbol with its appropriate sound, he is not making an automatic response. After practice, he will use distinctive features for recognition. At that point his conscious 'searching' will be for meaning across words, phrases and sentences. He is apt to stick on the conscious word-recognition level too long, either through lack of familiarity and practice or because he does not realise that he can make use of contextual cues.

SPEECH AND WRITTEN TEXT

The burden of the psycholinguistic message is that learning to read is part of the whole language experience of children in a society where the printed word is common. This implies that instruction should take the experience of spoken language which every child has into consideration from the start.

Text is not just 'speech written down' and it is sometimes difficult for children to make links between the two. The structures of speech and writing will vary, in that the written word uses a more formal register. Recent reading schemes often attempt to use the structures of spoken language so that the contextual cueing systems may be utilised easily (e.g. Berg *Nippers*, Reid *Link-up*). This does not always work as well as intended, although it is, of course, much better than the structures of early schemes which often bore no relationship to either normal spoken language or literary form.

Children accept easily that the vocabulary and form of stories is different from their own speech; for example, 'isn't' is written as 'is not' and 'he said' as 'said he'. What causes more trouble is the difference between marking and emphasis signals in speech and writing. Spoken intonational pattern and stress are probably the earliest features of language understood by young children. The stress system in English means that many of the vowel sounds are neutralised. We do not say every syllable in isolation, and the vowels in the unstressed syllables are heard as the 'er' sound. Words are not heard or said as isolated units, but in bunches of sounds which elide together. Here again, Downing's wish for 'cognitive clarity' is important, but it is difficult to know in what order to teach to achieve awareness. How do we know what a word is until we see it written down?

Punctuation, which replaces intonation in text, is a less sensitive marking system, and is ignored by learners at first because it is the spaces between words which are more obvious. In order to show real mastery of reading, a child must be able to transfer the written word into speech, used with natural intonation. Reading aloud is therefore necessary when learning in order to show the transition from word-by-word attack to this natural flow which indicates understanding.

In asking whether a person can read English we want to know, among other things, whether he can identify the question form from the clues he finds in writing, as evidenced by his use of oral intonation patterns that he has already learned are associated with questions in speech (Reed, 1970).

ORAL AND SILENT READING

There has been much less research done on silent reading than on reading aloud, except for a period in the nineteen-thirties when there were attempts to prove that it was possible, and advisable, to learn to read silently from the beginning. 'Silent reading as we know it was very rare until the advent of printing – in the ancient world books were used mainly for reading aloud, often by a slave' (Goody and Watt in Giglioli, 1972). Silent reading has usually been looked on as a 'second-stop' skill.

In England we have tended to believe that the ability to read silently will, however, automatically follow early reading aloud, and we also use the mistakes made in oral reading as an indication that a similar process will be operating in silent reading. Children are expected to go through the stages of 'mouthing' words and sub-vocalisation, (saying the words 'in their heads'), and many people think that mature silent reading is actually 'listening to words in the mind'.

There is a great deal of controversy and research into the question of whether the mature reader does sub-vocalise to some extent, and there is, as yet, little resolution of the arguments. A. Pugh's book *Silent Reading* marshals all the evidence on both sides:

> The view of the reader as a playback device or as a mere receptor of other men's words is restrictive, and in true silent reading he is not obliged to read in this way ... The skilled adult silent reader is not involved necessarily in a linear and sequential process akin to listening or oral reading (pp. 23–4).

Is there a qualitative difference between the two processes, or is it just that a mature reader has learnt to speed up his reading through experience? Certainly very proficient readers can read hundreds of words a minute, with adequate comprehension – far more words than they would be able to listen to and understand in the same time (400 words per minute is the maximum possible rate for speaking). Mattingly (Kavanagh and Mattingly, 1972) suggests that the fast reader can omit the intermediate stages of processing which a listener or beginning reader is going through.

Goodman (1968) suggests that eventually reading is 'visual' and that the graphic symbols can be encoded into messages which bypass the use of sound and listening. But he believes that children go through the in-between stage of noiseless listening-in. But even then the process is not necessarily a linear one of viewing the text, saying it silently to oneself and *then* coming to meaning. Elizabeth Hunter-Grundin (Hunter-Grundin 1979, p. 3) suggests a model which shows that 'decoding' and understanding are inter-related:

READING

| TEXT | ⟶ | TRANSLATION/ DECODING | ⟷ | UNDERSTANDING |

'Decoding' can certainly facilitate understanding, in the sense that the pronunciation of a letter configuration can help us to understand it. But the relationship can also operate the other way round. Understanding what a letter configuration means can help us to translate it correctly into speech sounds. For example, the letter combination 'row' is decoded one way if it has to do with 'moving a small boat forward' and in another way if it has to do with 'conflict or disagreement'.

The conclusion as far as the teacher is concerned is probably that children are likely to go through a 'listening' stage, but that ultimately good rapid reading should bypass the articulation of words, even in the head. Over-prolonged reading aloud while learning may make this more difficult to achieve. Training in use of varied reading rates, skimming, scanning and so on will probably be necessary to ensure that most people, even adults, become really efficient readers.

POINTS OF VIEW

The great amount of research on reading acquisition makes it difficult to select examples. Two writers have been chosen because what they say is particularly relevant to 'hearing children read', and because they have had a great influence on practice in the classroom in two different countries. The first researcher and teacher is Marie Clay, who has worked for many years in her native New Zealand. Her book *Reading: The Patterning of Complex Behaviour* (1972) is an invaluable practical handbook for teachers observing and diagnosing from oral reading.

Clay shows how even the beginning reader will have his own attitudes to books when he enters school, derived from home experiences. (Margaret Clark [1976] concluded similarly that exceptionally fluent readers came from the sort of home background [not necessarily middle-class] which encouraged children to take an interest in books.) Clay says how important it is to observe the child in the early stages, and to categorise the steps by which he comes to understand the arbitrary nature of print. The teacher listens, and corrects if necessary. Clay lists the concepts which the child may already have in some form when he comes to school, and suggests a developmental sequence arising from them:

Stage 1: Print can be turned into speech
The child makes up a phrase, or writes down a simple word that he knows and 'reads' it out – it will be what he 'thinks' he has written, and the 'reading' will demonstrate the child's own grammatical errors and collo-quial style.

Stage 2: A special type of talking
When he has heard stories read to him, the child will begin to adopt the 'story language' as he 'reads' a book. He has therefore begun to realise that the language there is different from his own and, indeed, different from anyone else's spoken language.

Stage 3: The picture is a guide to the message
The child makes up a statement which fits the book illustration but does not exactly coincide with the text.

Stage 4: Some sentences from the text are partially memorised
The child 'reads' by remembering captions and linking them with the illustration. He usually makes sentences which resemble the original text quite closely, and are in part identical to it.

Stage 5: Building a sentence word by word:
The child has realised that certain words keep on reappearing in his book; these are limited in number (e.g. Janet, John, come, look, the, up, etc). He makes sentences containing these words, still using picture clues as well. He is prepared (if the teacher tells him he is mistaken) to reformulate his theories until he is told he is correct. 'He is learning a vital link in early reading, to search, check, reformulate, correct and obtain some confirmation that he is right. He is not "reading" but he is learning how to process language information' (p. 31).

Even at this stage, Clay suggests that the child will make errors which make sense and which are grammatical. He is linking his hypothesising with his (implicit) knowledge of spoken language.

Clay then describes the child getting closer and closer to precise decoding, helped by the teacher's encouragement. The teacher helps by clarifying his own strategies for him – 'How did you know?' 'Where is the beginning of "-ive"?' 'Do you think you can find it somewhere else?' 'I'll run my fingers along the words – clap when you see "we" again' and so on.

The teacher will at the same time watch the child struggling with direction and the confusing identity of words and the spaces between them. She will observe the next breakthrough, which comes as an *apparent* retrogression – 'Fluency gives way to word-by-word reading. At that point the child over-emphasises the breaks between words and points with his finger. He has taken a major step . . . when his reading slows down and even becomes staccato. He may be thought of as "reading the spaces"' (p. 70). He is now integrating consciously three sets of behaviour – the words his eye sees, what his voice says and the direction of the print. It is interesting that at this stage the child's writing often shows an exaggerated space between words, so that he may only write three or four words on a line. He will begin, in his reading, to use correction devices which show that he is trying to match what his voice says to what he sees. He will realise that the text itself, not the picture, carries a message expressed in *one particular way*. Clay points out that the tentative processes of careful pointing and matching should give way to 'phrase reading' soon after the child starts on a reading scheme. It is nevertheless very important to observe and record the tactics he uses before he begins on his reading scheme, because if faulty strategies persist, (like over-use of pictures, 'making-up' the text) they may be difficult to eradicate.

Once the child is reading a book, Clay suggests keeping a running record of his achievement by asking him to read a *prepared* passage aloud. She sums up the strategies to watch for while this is happening:

Successful attack on words, errors, repetition, self-correction, the child's comments. Next in importance are his use of pointing, pause, directional errors and reading rate. In such observations the teacher is a 'recorder of behaviour and not a stimulus of behaviour – a guiding maxim would be "Record now; teach later"' (p. 104).

Clay shows that the teacher's guidance and reinforcement of what the child himself is contributing to the reading act is more important than direct sequential instruction.

The psycholinguists' view has been popularised by Frank Smith, and his first book *Understanding Reading* (Smith, 1978), was revolutionary in tone. He insists that reading is meaningful from the start. Children grow up assimilating spoken language in the context of events, and eventually attaching importance to and using only those collections of sounds which communicate a real message. 'As long as children see print as purposeless or nonsensical . . . they will be bored'. According to Smith, the process of prediction which has been used to produce and understand spoken language, must be transferred to print. By prediction, he means an awareness of relationships between textual units, an awareness of what is likely to occur, rather than a process of 'wild guessing'. It is possible to teach decoding skills by rote, but the child cannot generalise until he sees a reason for what he is doing.

Written language, says Smith, is different from oral in many ways, but most importantly, in the way it is verified. In everyday speech, verification of meaning is easy because it takes place in a mutually understood context.

With written language, difficult and possibly unique skills are required in order to verify, disambiguate and avoid error. Specifically, the skills involve following an argument, looking for internal consistencies, and thinking abstractly (Smith, op. cit.).

This seems a far cry from listening to children read, but even with early reading schemes it is possible to diagnose to some extent how far they are using these skills. The revolutionary aspect of Frank Smith's work lies in his insistence that the teacher's role should shift from direct instruction to supporting the pupils in finding their own ways into reading. It can be seen, therefore, that his conclusions are much the same as Marie Clay's. 'A child learns to read by reading and the teacher's role is to make reading easy . . . not by the use of simple material, which can indeed be difficult because of its probable irrelevance and unpredictability.' Rather, he suggests helping children to understand any written material which interests them – whether the help is provided by the teacher, an aide, another child, or a tape-recording – or simply by permitting children to *make errors and omissions without penalty* and without the disruption of unwanted correction (my italics).

Here can be seen the fundamental difference between the conventional practice of 'hearing children read' *in order to* prompt and correct, and the psycholinguistic view of the exercise. From the child's point of view, the reading aloud is seen to be exploratory, from the teacher's point of view, diagnostic. The motivational angle is also very important –

a child's commitment to learn reflects an economic decision made on the basis of cost and return . . . children who can make sense of instruction should learn to read, children confronted by nonsense are bound to fail. The issue is as simple – and as complicated – as that (op. cit. p. 116).

3 Reading aloud for a purpose

DIAGNOSIS

It is not surprising that reading aloud to the teacher has become such a widespread practice, as it is the most straightforward way of checking progress. It serves several purposes: the mistakes made indicate the reader's uncertainties, he can be given on-the-spot help, and there is direct social interaction between pupil and teacher. The seeming economy of such an apparently useful activity, however, may be over-estimated, as it is difficult to fulfil all purposes equally well at the same time. For instance, the ready help and instruction of the teacher may make the child over-reliant on her help and less ready to exercise his own faculties. What, of course, usually happens, is that he learns what ploys are expected of him and pays lip service (often literally) to carrying these out in order to win support and approval.

The practice is a necessary part of a teacher's work, and can be valuable if its functions are clearly delineated, and if it is realised that, paradoxically, in hearing a child read we are trying to wean him into reading *silently* as quickly as possible. We assume that the good strategies that we detect and encourage in oral reading will be transferred to mature silent reading. The next three chapters will look at ways in which listening to children read can be used economically and fruitfully.

Three main functions will be examined, with suggestions for their integration into the normal working life of the classroom. Oral reading may be used to *diagnose* how the child is progressing, to afford an opportunity for *instruction*, and what is often neglected today, to train the ability to read aloud for *communicative* purposes – to make a clear, if not necessarily dramatic, rendering of a text for listeners. Everyday practice has often led to the first two functions becoming confused, but it is important to differentiate them. Many teachers can carry out both simultaneously; a mistake in reading is registered mentally by the teacher, and instant feedback given to the pupil. Generations of practitioners seem to have found this a satisfactory exercise. Difficulties may arise, however; the interview with an individual child is usually very short (two to three minutes), and concentration on the reader and the text tends to be minimal, because of the many interruptions from other pupils seeking help. The teacher's reaction to a mistake may be largely intuitive, and it is all too easy to develop a style of response which emphasises one type of cueing. Until a teacher listens to herself in action she may not realise that she has become predominantly a 'prompter' or a 'sound-it-outer' or an over-zealous 'corrector'. The necessity to encourage children to use all the available cueing systems makes it advisable to diagnose the type of errors which are being made, in order to decide on appropriate teaching procedures. Acting also on the beliefs of Frank Smith, Goodman and others, that the child will actively solve his own problems, the teacher may decide that all the pupil needs is reinforcement for the positive strategies that he is exhibiting.

Diagnosis of strategies

We start from the assumption that when a 'mistake' is made in reading aloud – when the response differs in any way from the text – this does not happen by pure chance, but occurs for a psychological reason. Almost any reading matter can indicate, therefore, what causes deviation, but obviously mistakes are going to be more numerous and of a different kind if the text is too high a readability level for the learner.

The earliest standardised reading tests, for example Schonell's *Graded Word Reading Test* (1945) and Burt's *Word Recognition Test* (first published 1938), which demand single word recognition, can be used diagnostically, if, instead of merely scoring the number of errors, the tester examines them. A pattern may emerge where weaknesses of a particular type occur more than once. Information from such tests is very limited, however. Single word exposure does not allow for use of context, so that only one type of cueing system is available. It is better to take a passage from a current reader, which means that the material will vary from child to child. Diagnostic testing on this sort of text then becomes criterion- rather than norm-referenced. We are not testing what a reader can achieve in rela-tionship to others, but how he tackles a text which has some relevance for him. The *Neale Analysis of Reading Ability* (1958) may help here. It not only yields 'scores of a traditional nature', but also classifies reading errors, and is unique in England for this reason.

A series of complete short narratives is provided, graded for readability for children aged six to twelve years. Each passage is read, coded for errors, and accompanied by a set of comprehension questions.

This is only the bare bones of the examination. The area of a child's needs or his specific difficulties must be gained through alert observation of the way he reads, the items to which he responds, his attitudes, and more specifically, the errors he makes. This is likely to be done unsystematically if a record is not made at the time of testing (Neale, p. 6).

Final scores of fluency, accuracy and comprehension are calculable.

The *Neale Analysis* is still widely and profitably used, but mainly by remedial teachers and educational psychologists in cases of suspected reading retardation. Although it was first published well over twenty years ago, there is still no comparable test in Britain. American battery type tests, for example *Gates McKillop Diagnostic, Durrell Analysis of Reading Difficulty, Gilmore's Oral Reading* and *Gray's Oral Reading* (see Pumfrey, 1976), are the only other standardised tests which include assessment of oral reading errors in context. The types of error included for diagnosis vary, however, from test to test.

The *Neale Analysis* included many innovations, some of which were used in a different way in Goodman's *miscue analysis*. The first, already referred to, was the provision of graded passages rather than single words. Each test takes the form of a complete narrative, with an illustration: as Neale said, 'They transform the test into a picture story book which appeals more readily to the failing reader', and 'With some children they provoke spontaneous conversation which may be helpful to the examiner in recommendations for remedial work and reading materials' (Neale, op. cit., p. 7). Neale obviously thought that attitude to reading was important; the themes of the stories are varied and have not dated as much as some reading scheme material.

The second important innovation was the requirement to classify and record the errors made in the oral reading. Mispronunciations, substitutions, refusals, additions, omissions and reversals are categorised. Finally, though, a total score is made of errors, so that an accuracy level may be obtained. The implication is that only experts will use the test for diagnosis. There are thus profound differences between this test and miscue analysis; the test (as can be seen from the quotations above), was primarily intended to be administered to 'failing' readers, with the purpose of remediation. Errors, whatever their type, are indicators of weakness. The classification system is intended to allow 'more subtle assessments of weaknesses and strengths', but presumably the strengths are to be diagnosed from what the child gets *right*. Nevertheless, the test remains a very useful way of calculating levels of reading development.

Informal Reading Inventories

Informal Reading Inventories (I.R.I.) have become very popular in America, where they were first introduced by Betts (Betts and Welch, 1964) and since reported in various articles in this country, for example by Pikulski (in Chapman and Czerniewska, 1978) and Johnson and Kress (1965). They enable the teacher (*not* an examiner or tester) to diagnose the reading level which a child is attaining on a particular text. They have the advantage that the match between reader and text is surveyed; in this case the texts are not standardised passages, but are taken from the pupil's current reading material. 'The strength of the I.R.I. is not as a test instrument, but as a strategy for studying the behaviour of the learner in a reading situation and as a basis for instant diagnosis in the teaching environment' (Pikulski, op. cit. p. 353). Four functional levels of reading are suggested: Independent, Instructional, Frustration and Capacity. In practice, the Capacity level is rarely taken into account. The child reads aloud, and various factors are recorded: his accuracy in reading the words, his rate of reading, and his ability to answer questions on the text at different levels of comprehension. The table on the following page (reprinted from Pumfrey, 1977) shows how all these aspects can be percentaged and balanced with each other.

Independent reading means that the reader can cope on his own with the material, understands the passage, and remembers most of its content.
Instructional level means that he can read with help from the teacher where necessary.
Frustration level – The material is too difficult for him to cope with under any circumstances.
Capacity level – Reads material with over 75 per cent comprehension accuracy.

Although the I.R.I. has much to commend it overall, there are several difficulties implicit in the procedure. The first concerns what is meant by 'accuracy' in word recognition. What is to be counted as an error varies from writer to writer. In some cases, for instance, repetitions are counted as errors, in others not. More worryingly, as in the *Neale Analysis*, all errors are totalled together and counted as indicators of weakness, regardless of the fact that even mature readers make deviations from the original text in reading aloud. It is suggested that to attain Independent Reading Level on an average page of print (say 300 words), a child must make fewer than four errors; if his errors were meaningful substitutions, or small omissions that did not alter the sense, it would still mean that the passage was unsuitable for him to read without the teacher's help.

Another unexplained difficulty concerns the child who reads fluently

TABLE 2 SUGGESTED CRITERIA FOR ASSESSING SOME ACHIEVEMENTS USING AN INFORMAL READING INVENTORY

Skills Tested

Reading Level	Oral Reading Accuracy — i. flash presentation (i.e. ½" exposure)	Oral Reading Accuracy — ii. untimed	b. Words in context	Reading Comprehension — c. Definition of words out of context (text removed)	Reading Comprehension — d. Answering questions using contextual cues (text available)	Rate of Reading — e. Oral / f. Silent
Independent Level	90%-100%	95%-100%	99%-100%	90%-100%	90%-100%	Oral reading about half the rate of silent reading for same level of comprehension
Instructional Level	50%-89%	60%-94%	95%-98%	60%-89%	70%-89%	Oral reading rate equal to or not more than 15 words per minute *less* than silent reading
Frustration Level	Below 50%	Below 60%	Below 95%	Below 60%	Below 70%	Oral reading faster than silent reading by up to 15 words per minute
Capacity Level					Listening comprehension of 75% of materi‑	

(that is, with few errors), but who cannot satisfactorily answer questions on the text (or vice versa, which can occur surprisingly often). The I.R.I. states that reaching Frustration Level in *any one* of the categories means that the material is unsuitable.

R. A. McCracken (1964) adds some interesting dimensions to the I.R.I., as do Johnson and Kress (1965). These include observations of external behaviour which matches a particular reading level. For example, the Independent Behavioural Characteristics include 'rhythmical, expressive oral reading' and 'response to questions in language equivalent to author's'. It is arguable that understanding might be better demonstrated by the ability of the reader to use his own language in reply to questions! The Frustration Level characteristics include using 'an abnormally loud or soft voice', an 'unacceptable reading posture', and 'refusal to continue'. These criteria are evidently selected to obtain a profile of attitudes as well as skills, but they seem to be so subjective as to be positively misleading for some children. An avid reader may actually succeed in reading upside down!

So, although the idea of the I.R.I. is commendable, its over-structured provision of percentages and criteria for judging achievement pushes it back into the realms of time-consuming testing. The reading teacher in England is unlikely to use such detailed assessment. It is important, though, that she should develop a reliable instrument of her own for diagnosis, which will go beyond the bounds of subjectivity. Such an instrument could well be an adaptation of Kenneth Goodman's work on miscue analysis.

Miscue Analysis

This is a way of surmising what mental processes are in operation when a reader performs. This observation can only take place when the learner comes up against an obstacle in his reading and tries to surmount it, thereby making deviations from the original text. Goodman says that observing such strategies gives us 'a window on the reading process'. Two elements are observed; the first, the extent to which the reader makes an effort after meaning – that is, how far his errors continue to make sense – and second-ly, the success which he achieves in retelling what he has read.

Both emphasise the importance of understanding what is read, rather than of decoding words accurately. The reading is always from continuous text, and because the research was concerned with case-studies of children in school it is more relevant and accessible for teachers than much experimentally based reading research.

Goodman's theories are set out as a taxonomy in the 'Reading Research Quarterly' (1969). Many adaptations of the rather unwieldy machinery of analysis have been made, some of which will be described in the following pages. Goodman emphasises that miscue analysis is not a method of teaching reading but an aid to understanding the process of reading acquisition. 'What changes most is the perspective. But that is a pervasive change because it leads to a new set of criteria for judging what is of value in reading instruction ... process-centred, language-centred, meaning-centred'.

Goodman's approach is psycholinguistic (described in Chapter 2), and his method of analysing errors in oral reading fits into a theory rather than employing *ad hoc* methods designed primarily for remediation. His suggested analysis is highly complicated, and has been used mainly for in-depth case-studies of small numbers of readers, in order to clarify the processes of reading. A summary of the approach follows, to be preceded by some explanation of the underlying theory. Teachers can adapt Goodman's way of analysing in several ways for their own use, as long as they accept the underlying philosophy, which is basically at variance with the belief that the skills of reading can be mastered sequentially. The most readily available account of his thinking can be found in Frank Smith's *Psycholinguistics and Reading* (1973) to which Goodman contributed two chapters, 'Psycholinguistic Universals in the Reading Process' and 'Analysis of Oral Reading Miscues: Applied Psycholinguistics'.

In the first of these papers, Goodman differentiates between deep and surface levels of language. Although the reader must decode on the surface level (using his knowledge of sight-sound correspondence), his aim should be to get to the deep level of meaning. That statement may be misleading, as it implies an order, and a reader who is familiar with the type of material he is reading about could *start* with meaning, merely sampling and checking on the sight-sound level. He will carry out the reading act as economically as possible, sampling and predicting from the graphic display, using as few items as are necessary for his purposes. There are two implications: the first is that a 'mature' reader will handle text differently from one who has just learnt, and second, that his expectation of what is likely to be in the text will colour his reading and be determined by the perceptions which he brings to it. He may confirm or reject his expectations during this sampling procedure. 'The language user relies on strategies which yield the most reliable prediction with the minimum use of the information available' (Goodman, op. cit., p. 223).

Goodman believes that reading is not a precise process, and that decoding from the written word into sound is ultimately unnecessary. The skilled reader can derive meaning directly from the visual input, which is bound to be selectively perceived. An accurate decoding is not necessary, and can even at times handicap the direct reception of the message.

He explains how the three levels of language are used 'simultaneously and independently'. 'No readers read material they have not heard before without errors. It must be understood that in the reading process accurate use of all cues available would not only be slow and inefficient but would actually lead the reader away from his primary goal which is comprehension' (p. 26).

This theory turned upside-down attempts to gauge progress in reading by testing accurate word-recognition. Certain types of error indicate that the material has been absorbed, and that a re-encoding in slightly different language has been made. By analysing the types of error made, strategies can be deduced, which will indicate how far the reader has processed the available information. Goodman is at pains to show that no reader is 'mature' with all texts. When faced with difficult material, whose substance is beyond our experience, we all regress to sampling more carefully on the level of surface features, and thereby probably slow up our processing of the message.

The application of the theory to actual readers is qualitative rather than quantitative. Goodman has produced an intricate taxonomy, which enables the observer to calculate the balance in the use of the three levels of language. The main tenets of his system are listed below. Whatever adaptation a teacher makes in diagnosing pupils, it seems important to retain the principles.

1 A record is made of every response which differs from the original text, during oral reading of a passage. (E.R.= Expected Response; O.R. = actual, Observed Response)

2 Errors are known as *miscues*, to avoid the negative connotation of the word 'error'. Goodman diagnoses only from the miscues, not from the words read correctly. He believes that the way in which difficulties are tackled will, however, indicate the overall strategies in use. He also thinks that similar processes will operate in silent as in oral reading.

   Once the miscues have been recorded, the analysis is carried out by asking a number of questions about each miscue. 'The patterns which emerge produce a picture in depth of the reading process in the reader' (Goodman, in Smith, op. cit., p. 166)

3 Each miscue is examined according to the following criteria: Is it graphophonically similar to the text? Is it syntactically suitable? Does it make sense within the context of the whole passage? Three scores are obtained from these answers which may be balanced against each other. Various degrees of acceptability are considered.

4 Although the levels are coded separately, Goodman insists that they are sampled almost simultaneously. 'The reading process cannot be

fragmented . . . it is not in any sense a precise perceptual process' (p. 164).

5 Any reading matter must supply a full context to enable sampling to operate as it would in normal reading. ('Not flash cards or spelling material or phonic charts', p. 145.)

6 Special attention is given to correction by the reader of his own miscues. 'Perhaps the most significant factor in analysing any miscue is whether or not it was corrected' (p. 166).

7 Goodman recognises the interest of 'miscue chains'. Having made one mistake, a reader may deviate further from the text in order to 'get it all together'. This indicates a positive attack using the level of meaning.

8 The main categories other than self-corrections into which Goodman classifies miscues are: substitutions, insertions, omissions, reversals and refusals.

9 By analysing miscues in this way, it is possible to deduce, not only the decoding strategies of the reader, but whether he is reading for understanding.

Further measures can be carried out based on the same reading. Goodman extracts single words from the text and presents these before the passage is read as a whole. It is possible then to compare the error rate on single word presentation with the same words in context, and thus to see how far context is being utilised.

He also follows the reading by asking for free recall, with informal questioning about parts of the text which are not volunteered by the reader.

The reading should be tape-recorded, as it would be difficult to record the miscues accurately verbatim. Different symbols are used to code them on to a transcript. The passage should be taxing enough to set up some obstacles, preferably about a year above the child's reading age in a readability level. The aim is not to achieve a perfect reading; even an inexperienced, inaccurate reader may have 'got the message' – not only the literal message of the text, but the realisation that he has to bring his own knowledge to the reading.

This is a bare outline of Goodman's method. His analysis is too detailed to describe fully here, as teachers of full classes would have little opportunity to replicate it exactly. Some possible adaptations are described below. A simplified version will be illustrated in detail in the next chapter.

The R.M.I. (Reading Miscue Inventory) is set out in a manual by Yetta Goodman and Carolyn Burke (1972), devised 'to help the teacher understand how a reader's thought and language are brought to the reading task, and how a reader's experiences aid his interpretation of the author's meaning (p. 5). The resulting reader profile could provide the basis for a planned reading programme. Much useful knowledge can be gained even from a single reading.

The selected text should generate at least twenty-five miscues. The pupil is asked to read the passage without expecting help. On completion he is asked to retell the story in his own words. There are two final sources of information for the teacher, then: the Reader Profile and a Retelling Score (maximum 100 points).

The coding is carried out as Kenneth Goodman suggested, but with the addition of repetitions. Nine questions are asked of each miscue:

1 *Dialect* – Is a dialect variation involved?
2 *Intonation* – Is a shift in intonation involved?
3 *Graphic similarity* – How much does the miscue look like the stimulus word?
4 *Sound similarity* – How much does the miscue sound like the stimulus word?
5 *Grammatical function* – Is the grammatical function of the Observed Response the same as the Expected Response?
6 Is the miscue *Self-corrected*?
7 *Grammatical acceptability* – Does the miscue occur in a structure which is grammatically acceptable?
8 *Semantic acceptability* – Does the miscue occur in a structure which is semantically acceptable?
9 *Meaning change* – Does the miscue result in an overall change of meaning?

Again, it can be seen that the procedure is complex; it is clear from the questions that the rationale is the same as Kenneth Goodman's. The aim is to see how well the reader is balancing his strategies between (*a*) matching what he says to the look of the word and his phonic knowledge, (*b*) his use of syntactic experience and (*c*) his attempts to assign meaning to the text. The authors consider question nine to be the most important.

The methods for scoring the retelling of the story are interesting in that they indicate a broad way of carrying out discourse analysis. Marks are allocated for:

a) Character Analysis
b) Events – the actual happenings and the order in which they are recalled.
c) Plot – awareness of the *underlying* plan – the central concern of the story.
d) Theme – the viewpoint and generalised attitudes on which the story is built.

After the first attempt at unprompted recall, the teacher may probe gently with further questions which 'stimulate the student to expand', without actually feeding in further information.

The final results are percentaged and scores balanced against each other. The complexity of the reading process is emphasised, and the fact that there can be no accepted sequence in learning to read. 'You cannot know a process by listing its ingredients or labelling its parts; you must observe the effects of the parts as they interact with each other' (Goodman and Burke, op. cit., p. 45).

The teacher is recommended to concentrate on the strategies rather than the achieved skills of reading. 'Reading strategies are those interactions with written material which are available for the unaided reader'. The Manual gives suggestions for 'Reading Strategy Lessons' to help learners make their own sensible selection of strategies.

Miscue Analysis in Britain

Partly because of the complex nature of Goodman's work, it can only be used in a modified way in the classroom. Educationists in this country have devised adaptations of the approach, keeping the theory intact, which are more feasible for general use. Only brief mention will be made of them here, as their findings are readily available in this country.

The most accessible account is Elizabeth Goodacre's manual *Hearing Children Read* (1979), which not only explains a simplified procedure, but includes a useful annotated bibliography of relevant research. Goodacre mentions, for instance, the classic study by Biemiller (1970), which observed the oral reading errors of seven-year-olds, and isolated the stages that children pass through in learning to read. Great emphasis is placed on self-correction as a crucial stage in passing from 'learning to read' to 'reading to learn'.

Pumfrey looked at informal reading inventories and error analysis from a different angle (1977). He recommended that the use made of context cues could serve as a useful guide to progress. Each context cue could be examined in three ways: first, to see how far the child had used preceding and succeeding context in overcoming an obstacle, evidenced by a miscue; second, to see whether he was restricting his understanding to the sentence being read, or third if he was incorporating outside experience. He suggests ways of encouraging pupils to use context cues, which will be mentioned in Chapter 5.

Another way of using miscue analysis has been put forward by Donald Moyle (Raggett *et al.*, 1979). Miscues are categorised in ten possible classes, and then transferred to a matrix which is marked out in squares. The grid allows the teacher to see at a glance which miscues are 'good' in that they show reading for meaning. The grid indicates to a certain extent whether the reading material is too hard for the child. 'Many other conclusions can be drawn by observing the weightings of errors within various categories' (p. 81). The same book includes a case study account by Jenny Senior, describing an attempt to use an Informal Reading Inventory and miscue analysis with Michael, an easily distracted reader of 9 years old (p. 80).

Miscue analysis is now finding its way into the teachers' manuals of commercial reading schemes. A case in point is *Reading 360*, published by Ginn, which includes an excellent summary by Adrienne Jack (Levels 5 and 6, p. 28). In spite of this, it is surprising that the chapter does not appear till four 'levels' have already been covered, and that it is surrounded, fore and aft, by many 'decoding activities' based on strictly phonic rules. So, the summary itself says admirably, 'The most important graphophonic information for a reader is the first one or two letters of a word. Followed by the final letter, they are often the only graphic cues used to *predict* a word. This limited use of graphic/sound cues produces successful reading when it supports the use of grammatical and meaning cues' (p. 38). This is followed however, by some very intensive training on vowel and vowel-consonant digraphs, and the pattern of activities is sequentially divided into 'decoding', 'extension' and 'comprehension' tasks. It is important that the spirit behind miscue analysis is preserved, which is that the reader should use all cueing systems interchangeably, and that learning will best occur using meaningful text.

SHARING THE READING ACT

Diagnosis of reading progress does not always come from the close analysis of errors which we have described. All teachers make judgements on the capabilities and potentialities of their pupils by observing their attitudes and their ways of tackling tasks. This is legitimately part of the teacher's art and sensitivity. Because such judgements are often intuitive, as many teachers will admit, there is a danger that a strong opinion may be formed on the basis of scanty evidence, which is then perpetuated. It is all too easy to label a child as 'bright' or 'remedial' and for the resulting self-fulfilling prophecy to ensure that such labels become 'real'.

What is needed is to focus these broader ways of diagnosing behaviour, to become consciously aware of their importance, and to be sure that one is constantly reappraising the child. This section will describe some of the 'ways of looking' which can be used during oral reading, in order to help teachers to develop clear focusing procedures. Inevitably now, diagnosis merges into teaching; the interaction between teacher and taught is the richest learning situation, the shared experience which arises out of the teacher's observation of the total reading act and her subsequent discussion with her pupil.

Observing reading behaviour: Attitudes and developmental approaches

Much can be learnt about attitudes to reading without questioning the child directly. The transcript of a tape-recorded reading can yield information which cannot be quantitatively measured, but which is nevertheless valuable. The occasions on which a child 'refuses' to try words will, for example, indicate his approach to the task. It may be that he does not realise that he should be trying to solve his own problems, because he has always been prompted quickly. 'Wild' guesses indicate, perhaps, a child who believes he should keep going at all costs. Repetitions of words, and hesitations before them, may show different attitudes towards reading. The 'repeater' is often more successful than the 'hesitator'. He may repeat an easy word which occurs just before the one causing difficulty, in order to keep the flow of language going, just as a speaker often inserts meaningless tag items, 'I mean', 'You know', while his thoughts click into place for his next statement. Repetitions may serve another purpose; if a child repeats a word which is probably new to him, or unexpected in the context, it will be to verify for himself that he is right, thus indicating a careful reader, anxious to derive meaning from the text. As in so many of the phenomena already mentioned, the way of responding may include developmental as well as personal factors. Mavis Hilton found in her M.A. study (Unpublished thesis, Lancaster University 1975) that young children from 5.9–6.0 years did not often repeat a word previous to the one causing difficulty.

'Hesitators' are often less aware of meaning than 'repeaters', and may be anxious to get every word right. They may have little idea of the real purpose of reading. When such children are asked why they think learning to read is necessary, they will often venture such answers as 'It helps you to learn new words' or 'It helps you to spell'. With both hesitations and repetitions which are made before a difficult word, some indication can be gained of eye-voice span (the amount of text which is absorbed in one eye-movement). With beginning or unsure readers, the hesitation or repetition will occur immediately before the word causing difficulty, whereas with more able practitioners it may occur several words earlier.

Researchers have noted rate of reading as an important diagnostic feature, some even timing the words read with a stop-watch. This does not seem very useful, as even adult readers will vary in their reading rate. The overall pace is interesting, however, and even more helpful to observe is the child's ability to read with natural intonation and not word-by-word. Many teachers have noticed that this often seems to happen almost overnight. It is as if a click of recognition enables the learner to 'read for meaning'. This must be the tip of the iceberg, the time when, through practice, words are recognised automatically on the surface level, so that the full attention can be given to deep structure. It certainly seems to be a clearly observable landmark in reading development.

Closely linked to this facility is the ability to observe the conventions of Juncture, Pitch and Stress; (those sensitive to juncture will stop suitably at the end of phrases and sentences). Intonation is one of the earliest features of spoken language to carry meaning for the infant listener. Written language is much more difficult to split up, since punctuation rarely marks more than juncture and the most obvious intonation and speech patterns (questions, exclamation marks, inverted commas and so on). In order to put the correct stresses and vocal patterning into an oral reading, the deep structure must be appreciated. It is understandably late in the development of reading skill that children begin to make their reading sound like natural speech. Conflicting motivations can operate at all stages; in early reading the child is anxious to get every word right and will be unlikely to be able to look along the line to 'chunk' phrases. At the other extreme, a skilled reader who is asked to read aloud may use a flat neutral intonation to approximate to the speed of silent reading. Holdaway (1972) says that before a reader can convey orally the difference between such sentences as

'Oh no! That would happen.'
'Oh no? Who does he think he is?'
'I think it was blue. Oh no – now I remember – it was green.'

he must realise the deep structure of the whole utterance. Holdaway shows, interestingly, that the tone of the writing may push the reader into using varied stress patterns. For instance, 'When we take a sentence out of context there is seldom call to read it in any but the neutral manner, for example:

'He was a little boy.'

But when we place this sentence in a wider context, we find that it is almost impossible to read in the neutral manner:

'Poor Herman. He wasn't a bear. He was a little boy.'

Holdaway says that three items of knowledge are necessary before such sentences are read with natural intonation: the child must know what he is reading about, he must know the conventions of punctuation, and he must have heard similar structures spoken.

We can see the importance of good reading by an adult to children, as a model; and how unhelpful many early reading schemes are, using as they do patterns of sentence which are unlikely to be heard in any society.

Marie Clay's research (1971) into the relationship between accurate reading and correct use of pause and stress showed that the children who paused least (that is, who observed the 'normal' phrase-patterning) were also the most accurate readers. The best readers also paused more briefly and completed sentences with a fall in pitch. 'The poorer reader was more likely to use a rising or sustained pitch, implying uncertainty. The poorer readers also used far more heavy stresses, with the very inaccurate readers using 1.1 stresses *per word*, as if they were reading out a list of words.' Clay realised that it is difficult to draw simple cause-and-effect conclusions, but that it is likely that good readers 'can work through a sequence of possibilities guided by story, intersentence and sentence cues, and can drop to the levels of phrase, word and letter probabilities if necessary.' It is interesting that the emphasis put on word by word reading by the poorer readers did *not* make them more accurate readers – in fact, the longer they took to read, the less accurate they were.

It is clear that observing these features during the oral reading activity can be a useful indication of reading development. Clay's work is particularly important because it encourages us, not only to diagnose within the sentence, but to observe strategies which indicate how the child is dealing with the whole continuity of narrative.

As has been explained above, diagnosis can be supported by the request for recall after the oral reading. But it is not so much the reproduction of the actual facts which is important, but the way that the recall is organised. If the reader rewords the language of the original in his own language, this must surely demonstrate that he is re-encoding substance which he has assimilated, rather than repeating the original by rote. It is fascinating to look at the information which he does *not* reproduce during the immediate recall session, but which may rise to the surface with subsequent probing; often a word or a phrase from the teacher will trigger off a whole new series of recalled facts.

It is also useful to observe how far the reader supplies his own 'gloss' on the remembered episode. He may comment critically or appreciatively, showing that his judgement has been at work during the reading. Alternatively, he may show that he has made faulty associations of meaning. This often happens when figurative language is used, which the child is unlikely to have heard in speech. In reading a passage including the phrase 'He had to duck to avoid the huge white wings' (see Chapter 4), one reader of eight had trouble reading the sentence, not because she did not recognise the word 'duck', but because its metaphorical use was confusing, particularly in a sentence that was referring to an *un*metaphorical bird! Sure enough, when she came to tell the story in her own words, she jumped to the (wrong) conclusion that the bird in question was a duck.

We often observe the child's success in retaining the original sequence in the retelling of a story, and are impressed by the accuracy of order in which the events are told. However, this is not always an infallible guide to good reading. Sometimes an understanding reader will re-arrange the sequence, selecting what seem to him the most important aspects, and relegating the unimportant to parentheses. In many ways, therefore, to ask for retelling is a surer guide to understanding than the teacher's direct questioning, since her questions must reflect *her* understanding of the story, which is not necessarily the only interpretation.

Observing reading behaviour: styles of reading

Up to now, we have been concerned with diagnosis directly connected with the oral reading of a particular text. A single reading will also display many features which demonstrate the child's overall attitudes and styles of learning. Some of these will be clearly related to the interaction with the teacher, and may have become habitual responses through fulfilled expectations. For instance, a child who initially lacked confidence in word-attack skills may have found the teacher ready to prompt quickly on each hesitation. He may have become over-dependent, unwilling to hypothesise, waiting for help. Other children may be anxious not to appear as poor readers, and will anxiously hazard guesses, usually employing only the first phoneme of a word as a cue. Concentration – or the lack of it – is again easily observable from a transcript of miscues. There is often a recurring pattern; sometimes the beginning of a read is hesitant and careful, whereas the last paragraph or so shows greater speed and more errors. Self-corrections may diminish as the reader tires. On the other hand, some readers take time to 'get into the passage', showing increasing concentration as they progress through it.

Brickett (1979) gives some useful pointers to different cognitive styles, which may affect reading. She quotes Bruner's categorisation of learners into 'conservative focussers' and 'gambling focussers'. 'Conservative' learners tend to learn details first and are slow to synthesise, while 'gamblers' take chances and jump to conclusions.

R. Gardner (she quotes) uses Gestalt terminology, isolating 'levellers' and 'sharpeners'. A learner who sharpens tends to remember details better than the total context, while levellers remember the total situation. More well-known are Kagan's categories of 'impulsive' and 'reflective' learners, who will adopt different styles of approach which will tend to be either 'thematic' or 'analytic'.

A useful summing up of different categories of cognitive styles is that of C. M. Charles (1980). He suggests that three distinct ways of approaching learning situations are apparent in learners; he describes the clusters of behaviour associated with these classifications:

'Adventurers' – very active, alert, eager, curious
– anxious to try out every new activity, explore every new idea
– self starters who work well on their own
– do not require much support and encouragement
– work creatively
– do not pay close attention to detail
– often leave activities incomplete in their eagerness to move on to others

'Ponderers' – start more slowly but persevere longer
– like structure, pay attention to details
– seek positive feedback which can come from self-checking
– concerned about 'right' way and 'right' answers
– have a sense of direction and accomplishment
– produce high quality work

'Drifters' – like the physical presence of teacher or adult both in getting started and throughout activity
– like structure and constant feedback from teacher
– sometimes require extrinsic rewards to keep them at a task
– easily distracted
– require support of classmates
– follow directions well
– like routines

Although these apply to general styles of learning, there is evidently a direct and easily perceivable relationship with the ways in which children approach reading. Hilton found (op. cit., 1975) in assessing reading development of five to six year olds, that school experience, teaching method and tested reading ability did not account for all the differences between children's reading. She hypothesised a Reading Style, which would probably link closely with cognitive style, and also to personality traits. It seems important to accept the existence of such styles, and to encourage the 'good' elements in each by working on strengths and enthusiasms.

Observing reading behaviour: children's concepts about reading

Diagnosis is often thought of as the observer's prerogative, but even young children can show insights into their own reading processes if sympathetically consulted. Much of the evidence in this section comes from the reading interviews which were conducted with seven to nine year olds in the *Extending Beginning Reading* Project (Southgate *et al.*, 1981). The format for the interviewing was based on Jessie Reid's research *Thirteen Beginners in Reading* (Reid 1958). Such interviews could well supplement, or occasionally replace, the practice of hearing a child read. Although it would be impossible to hold frequent interviews with individuals, one in-depth talk could yield a great deal of evidence to enable a programme to be planned for some time ahead.

Each child is asked to bring two books with him; the book he is reading to the teacher and his current self-selected book. The discussion is best kept as informal as possible, with the basic framework of questions allowing for expansion and anecdote. Four aspects are described below: the child's understanding of the nature of reading, his own interpretation of the strategies in use, his evaluation of himself as a reader and his awareness of the function of reading both with regard to himself and others.

THE NATURE OF READING

Children may be confused about the nature of reading on many levels, from the surface features of letters, words, spaces between words and so on, to a total lack of awareness of what makes the differences between speech and writing. Jean-Paul Sartre (1967) vividly describes his first experiences of being read to by his mother:

> She leant over, lowered her eyelids and went to sleep. From this mask-like face issued a plaster voice. I grew bewildered: who was talking? about what? and to whom? . . . And then I did not recognise the language. Where did she get her confidence? After a moment, I realised it was the book that was talking. Sentences emerged that frightened me; they were like centipedes; they swarmed with syllables and letters, spat out their diphthongs and made their double consonants hum; fluting, nasal, broken up with sighs and pauses, they were in love with themselves and their meanderings and had no time for me: sometimes they disappeared before I could understand them. . . . These words were obviously not meant for me (p. 31).

Reid's questioning of twelve five-year-olds (1966) revealed similar impressions, which were confirmed by Downing (Chapman *et al.*, 1978). When asked 'What is in books?' young children mentioned pictures, names of characters, or specific phrases or sentences, very rarely 'writing' or 'words'. Strangely, they did not think of books as containing stories, or information. Children in Downing's sample were asked, 'Do books have stories in them?' Seven agreed that they did (out of thirteen), but this, it appeared, usually meant stories that were read to them by an adult.

There is a close link here with the answers to the questions 'Do you need to learn to read? Why?' which were asked in the *Extending Beginning Reading* project (Southgate *et al.*, 1981). Most children thought they should, but their reasons were mainly that it 'would help you to learn words', 'helps with spelling' or 'stops you getting into trouble when you get to secondary school'. Eight children (out of forty-one) mentioned that it could give information, but only three of the total sample mentioned that learning to read could give pleasure.

It seems that there is, with many young learners, an inability to link the reading that they hear as enjoyable narrative with the reading that they *do*, which seems to them mastery of a purposeless skill. This was seen at its most extreme in one seven-year-old's reply to the above questions. He thought one should learn to read; when asked 'Why?' he replied, 'Then I can stop'. Obviously a child like Peter, who replied 'It's a lot more exciting than just writing. You get things that are going to be exciting in a minute', had a concept of reading which is likely to prove much more fruitful. Unfortunately, he appeared to be in a minority.

Children proved equally vague when asked to say what a 'letter' and a 'word' were. It is difficult to define these verbally, but reasonable to ask children to point to or pick out letters or words. Teachers sometimes use technical terms (words describing features of language) without being sure that pupils really understand what they are referring to. Downing (op. cit.) thinks that this may lead to children accepting reading as 'a kind of ritual which they have to perform to please adults . . . Many children take a very long time to learn the essential truth about reading which is that it is to convey interesting information to the reader' (p. 240).

CHILDREN'S DESCRIPTIONS OF STRATEGIES

Confusion and ritualised response are equally evident when children are asked what they consider difficult in reading, and what they do to overcome problems.

Marie Clay (1972, p. 172) asked a sample of children 'What do you do when you come to a word you don't know?' The table reproduced below shows the emergent conscious analysis from ages seven to eight. The categories given are in themselves an interesting guide to the possible ways in to overcoming obstacles in word-recognition.

TABLE 3

Response	7 year-olds (N100)	8 year-olds (N50)
	%	%
I don't know	29	–
Say the word in parts	23	65
Miss it out and go to the end	15	4
Look at the beginning	7	10
Look for little words in big words	3	6
Spell it	5	8
Work it out, think it up	8	–
Write it down	4	–
Ask the teacher	3	–
Look at the picture	2	–

From Clay (1972) *Reading: the Patterning of Complex Behaviour*

Both Reid (1958) and Southgate *et al.* found that children thought that it was 'hard words' which made books difficult. Older children elaborated a little by quoting such features as 'small print' and 'long stories'. The ways of answering 'What do you do when you come to a difficult word?' differed from Clay's results in that the most frequent response was 'Ask the teacher'. This is unlikely to be true in practice, but it is interesting that the sample (Southgate's) probably felt that it was the *right* thing to do. In other words, dependence is, they think, more laudable than self-help devices. Frequently mentioned were tactics like 'sounding it out', and 'spelling it', all showing a belief that sound-symbol matching was paramount. Like Clay's sample, very few children volunteered that they 'guessed' a word, and hardly any admitted to missing a word out. The child therefore, on the whole, thinks of reading analytically, and is not consciously aware of the acceptability, and indeed, the necessity, of using context cues.

Such questions, then, may be helpful not only in diagnosing what children think they do in reading, but by extrapolation, in bringing out the teaching emphasis, which may have become unbalanced. It is quite feasible for beginning readers to be told through demonstration and example that there are several cueing systems which they can use.

It may be, of course, that the child, in answering, associates the word 'reading' with the *skill* rather than its use, and so does not mention understanding, function, or enjoyment, because he thinks they are not relevant to the question. This in itself is interesting, since it would indicate a disassociation between decoding and reading for meaning.

Child's evaluation of himself as a reader

To ask the question 'Do you think you are a good reader?' of a young learner is to invite answers which will reflect the ·child's notion of what constitutes reading, as well as his – perhaps not always honest – evaluation of his own skill. When a second question follows, 'Why do you think so?' strange laws of cause and effect are revealed. In this type of questioning, the child will probably give answers which he thinks the teacher will want.

In the 'Extending Beginning Reading' project, half the sample thought they were good readers, one third were doubtful, and only seven children were sure that they were not good readers. The reasons for their judgements fell within the following categories:

1 Those who felt that they were able or unable to tackle reading *as a skill*. They referred to word recognition – 'There aren't many words I don't know' and 'Well, I'm a bit good – I sometimes get stuck on words, but I don't get stuck on all of them'. They did not think of reading as mastery of overall strategies, nor did they mention the element of comprehension. Nor did they come to the conclusion that their book might be too difficult for their stage of development. Their reasons linked closely with teachers' evaluations of good readers, when the criterion was usually 'fluent oral reading' (for example, 'a fluent reader, but poor at comprehension').

2 They frequently evaluated themselves in relation to other children, reflecting the competitive, extrinsically-motivated aura which pervades early reading acquisition. For example, one boy commented, 'Some people are on higher and some on lower books'. The judgements were not made as a result of hearing each other reading, but by comparing the texts they were on. When asked 'Are some people better than you?' a nine-year-old girl answered, 'Yes, because some are on library books and they're all past me. They're not on *Wide Range*.' Others evaluated themselves according to the group they had been allocated to, or the teacher's assessment, for example, 'I'm almost bottom. Mrs H. has got a chart and you see your name, whether you're first, second, third, fourth, fifth, sixth, seventh. It depends how you read when she comes round to the group.'

3 Some children were influenced in their judgement by the opinion of

people at home: 'I read every night to my mother and she says I'm quite good' and 'My uncle says I can read like an eleven-year-old' (a nine-year-old girl).

4 Another reason for high self-evaluation was the amount that was read, although this tended to be mentioned more by nine-year-olds. Thick books and small print seemed to become at that stage symbols of achievement, and the older children felt themselves to be mature readers when they were allowed to choose such books for themselves.

It would be interesting to trace a child's growth of belief in himself as a reader by recording his answers across the formative years, and to notice the point, which one hopes would come for most children, when they realise that their success in reading varies according to their familiarity with the material. Many may come to the equally important conclusion that reading well means 'understanding' and 'assimilating' the content of what is read. On the evidence of the project, such evaluations only emerge about the age of nine.

THE FUNCTION OF READING

Jessie Reid (op. cit., 1958) whose sample was 5–6 year old boys, asked a set of questions concerning the purpose of reading, including queries about children's ideas on adult reading. All the children thought about the far-distant future when they would be able to read newspapers or books. They seemed vague about their parents' reading; some were not even sure whether their parents could, as one child termed it, 'read into themselves' without 'saying it out loud'. The older children in the 'Extending Beginning Reading' project gave very different answers. They knew what silent reading was, and two-thirds of them preferred it to reading out loud to the teacher. One second year girl showed a mature approach by saying, 'When you read to other people, it makes you go slower and you always stop on words you might not know when you do it in your mind'.

There was a curious dissociation in the reading function as they saw it for themselves and for adults. Whereas it has been shown that they did not on the whole see their own reading as other than mastery of the decoding skills, they were very sensible of the ways their parents used reading. They knew when newspapers, magazines, romances and 'rude books' were read, and that it also helped when 'Dad was reading how to mend the car' and 'Mum reading cookery books'. So the functions of reading, as they saw them, were very different for themselves and for their relatives.

We have tried to show how valuable informal discussion can be in diagnosing underlying assumptions about reading, from the awareness of the symbolic system to its myriad purposes. Cashdan (1969) believes that there is often a gap in children's understanding of 'the totality of reading experience', and this is often because of the lack of 'verbal mediation'. We need to talk to children about the process, gradually introducing the vocabulary which is needed to describe it *as* a process, so that the child does not pick up the myths of a 'conventional wisdom' which has not become conventional for him, and perhaps never will.

It is clear that psycholinguists and cognitive psychologists believe that knowing *how* learning is achieved is equally important as checking that it has occurred. Rothkopf (1972) sums this up admirably. He says that trying to match a text to the supposed reading level of the child does not necessarily tell us what is being learnt. The way the learner approaches the task is just as important. His reasons for reading, his attitudes to it, the way he tackles it and the environment in which it occurs, will all influence his understanding of what is read. Rothkopf calls these 'mathemagenic activities'. It is apparent that, in forming their strategies for reading, children may have vague ideas about what they *should* do, when what they actually *do* may be different. This is where the reading interview, and a very clear if simple exposition of what is involved in reading, may encourage the right strategies and suitable attitudes.

The format of interview used in the 'Extending Beginning Reading' project is quoted below, for guidance to teachers structuring their own diagnostic reading interviews. The questions need not be asked in order, or in the original wording.

CHILD INTERVIEW – RECORD FORM

Child's views on own reading

1 Do you like reading?
   Why do you like to read? or What do you like about it?
2 Do you think you are a good reader?
   What makes you think that?
3 Do you prefer to read quietly to yourself or to read aloud to someone?
   Why is that?
4 Do you read a lot at home? More than at school?
5 What kind of books do you like best?
6 Where do you get the books from?

7 Do the people at home read much?
8 What sort of things do they read?

Child's view of reading difficulties

1 What made you choose this book? (self-chosen book)
2 Is it a difficult (hard) book?
3 Is it more difficult or not so difficult as the book you are reading with your teacher?
4 What makes a book difficult?
5 Show me a difficult word. What makes it hard?
6 If you come to a word you don't know, when you are reading by yourself, what do you do?

The purpose of reading

1 Do you think children should learn to read? Why/Why not?
2 Why do you think grown-ups need to be able to read?

From Southgate *et al.* (1981) *Extending Beginning Reading*

4 Miscue analysis in the classroom

It has been suggested that diagnosis of reading strategies may usefully be made from an examination of errors in oral reading. We have also suggested that the methods of analysis used by researchers are complex and time-consuming. Some teachers say that they gain more (after studying such methods) from their changed attitudes towards reading instruction than by carrying out full-scale diagnostic exercises in their classrooms. Other teachers, though, have invented their own simplified versions of miscue analysis, which have proved useful in many ways. This chapter suggests a modified method of analysing miscues which should be feasible for general use. It has been discussed with many groups of teachers, who have helped in its development and have been encouraging about its possibilities. This method will be described step by step, and will be illustrated by examples showing its use with children at different stages of reading development.

1. Choose a passage (narrative or non-fiction), about 150–300 words long, which is likely to tax the reader without frustrating him. Up to a reading age of 6+ it is quite possible to use the child's current reader, since he is likely to be making sufficient deviations to make diagnosis possible; above a reading age of about 6+, a readability level of 9–12 months higher than the child's 'normal' reading is suggested. If possible, duplicate the passage (reasons for this and alternatives will be given later).

2. Tape-record the reading, having said to the child something like: 'I want you to read this to me as well as you can. I would like to see how well you can manage without me helping you, so keep going, and I'll only tell you a word if you get really stuck. We are going to tape-record your reading, so let's say your name and how old you are before you begin'.

3. Code the miscues on to the duplicate passage as shown opposite.

The reading must be tape-recorded, partly because it is often necessary to replay it in order to code accurately, and partly because it might be off-putting to the reader to make notes during the activity.

4. The coded transcript of this particular reading (Angus: 8 years 2 months) appears on pp. 61–2.

MISCUE TYPE	ORIGINAL TEXT	ACTUAL RESPONSE	CODING SYMBOL
Non-response (refusal)	prairie	no attempt to say any part of word	<u>prairie</u>
Substitution	which crept between his toes	which kept betwen his toes	which crept ^{kept} between his toes
Omission	I feel like a grease-spot	I feel like grease-spot	I feel like ⓐ grease-spot
Insertion	and then found he couldn't stop	and then he found he couldn't stop	and then found he couldn't stop
Reversal	so tightly was he pinned down	so tightly he was pinned down	so tightly was he pinned down
Self-correction	then the laughing turned	then he-the laughing turned	then the laughing turned
Hesitation	so wide that	Hesitates for some time then supplies word. Oblique stroke shows where hesitation occurs.	so wide/that
Repetition	Thomas tried to break the threads	Thomas tried to tried to break the threads	Thomas <u>tried to</u> break the threads

ATTACKED BY INSECTS

1 The great <u>prairie</u> was so wide that the two boys could see nothing but miles
of yellow earth.

    "I feel like ⓐ grease-spot", said Mark, taking off his <u>anorak</u>, shoes and
socks. The minute his bare feet touched the ground they were covered by
5 thousands of tiny insects <u>which</u> crept between his toes and tickled him
under his feet.

He began to laugh, and then found he couldn't stop. He rolled over
and over on the ground and the little insects soon covered him completely.
One got into his ear and he laughed even more. Then the laughing turned
10   into squeals of panic. The insects were pushing out little threads from their
bodies which fixed Mark to the ground. Soon he could not move, so tightly
was he pinned down. Thomas tried to break the threads, but they were as
strong as nylon.
    "Lie absolutely still", he ordered Mark, "and for goodness sake stop
15   yelling".
    Suddenly a bird flapped overhead and darted down towards the boys.
Thomas had to duck to avoid the huge white wings. Then he saw that the
bird was pecking at the threads to break them in two. The insects
disappeared into the ground when they saw the bird's threatening beak.

5. An overall impression of the number of errors can be gained from
looking at this transcript, but in order to see what strategies are being used,
further classification is necessary. The main aim is to discover the balance
between *positive* and *negative* strategies. Positive strategies evidence the
child's attempts to read for meaning, and are usually demonstrated by the
same sort of mistakes that an adult reader might make. Negative strategies
are typified by immature errors, showing little attempt at successful
word-attack.

The following grid should be filled in (leaving substitutions till last, since
they offer added information – see below, page 64). Angus's mistakes have
been entered; the reasons for the decisions follow.

Type of miscue	Non-response	Substitution	Omission	Insertion	Reversal	Self correction	Totals
1 Positive	–	6	1	2	2	3	14
2 Negative	2	4	1	–	–	1	8

Hesitations and repetitions are not included in the general grid, as they
show styles of reading rather than strategies (see page 48ff.).

GUIDANCE ON CODING

Non-responses

If the reader is unable to use any word-attack skills and waits (often anxiously) for prompting, his strategy is bound to be negative. In this case, therefore, the two non-responses, prairie and anorak are coded in column 2 (Negative).

Omissions and Insertions

These are the types of error which a mature reader will often make, indicating that he has assimilated the original language and adapted it slightly into his own language-patterns on re-encoding in speech. Such miscues will most likely be small words which do not alter the sense of the original, in which case they exemplify positive strategies, and should be coded in Column 1. Sometimes, of course, a beginning reader will omit words for less positive reasons, (for example he may skip a word because he does not recognise it), and this type of omission will be coded negatively. In the sample text, the *omissions* were –

I feel like ⓐ grease-spot – *Negative*, because it makes the sentence grammatically wrong.

He rolled over (and over) on the ground – *Positive*, because the second 'and over' is redundant. Omission does not seriously destroy sense.

Insertions

and then ʰᵉ found he couldn't stop – *Positive* – makes no difference to sense.

One got into his ear and ᵗʰᵉⁿ he – *Positive* – supplying for himself laughed even more   a perfectly reasonable adverb.

Reversals

(NB Reversals of *words*, rather than letters within words, which would be coded as substitutions). These may be positive or negative. They are not found frequently in beginning readers. In the sample text:

taking off his anorak,

    shoes and socks   – *Positive* – no change of meaning.

so tightly was he pinned down – *Positive* – a re-encoding in language closer to speech.

Self-corrections

As described in Chapter 3, self-corrections become frequent at around a Reading Age of 8 to 9, and diminish thereafter. (NB Code all miscues which are self-corrected twice, once for original error, and then as a self-correction.)

If a child realises he has made a mistake and goes back to correct it, it indicates that he is reading for meaning, usually a positive strategy. Not always, however. In two cases, the self-correction will be negative: (*a*) if he corrects with the wrong word and (*b*) if he corrects on a miscue which does not alter the original meaning. Goodman calls this over-correction, and Angus exemplifies this when he corrects his original reversal 'socks and shoes', quite unnecessarily. His self-corrections are coded thus:

the two boys could ~~see~~ ^{not ✓} nothing   *Positive* – original error syntactically wrong

taking off his anorak, shoes✓and socks   *Negative* – over-correction

which ^{kept ✓} ~~crept~~ between his toes   *Positive* – sense was wrong in original response

Then ~~the~~ ^{he ✓} laughing turned into squeals of panic   *Positive* – realisation that 'laughing' is used nominally, not as a verb.

Substitutions

These probably yield more information than any other type of miscue, and could indeed be fruitfully examined in isolation. Rebecca Barrs (Chapman and Czierwska, 1978) sums up their importance. She says that they are frequently not random guesses but calculated responses gained from different cues. She assumes that substitutions reflect more than anything else the system which is at work when readers make successful responses. She found that the substituted words are often those which have already been met in reading, not from spoken vocabulary items, particularly when children have initially been taught by whole-word methods. Those who have been taught with a phonic emphasis tend to offer 'nonsense' substitutions. Substitutions therefore often indicate memorising and consolidating strategies – the attempt to utilise old knowledge to solve a new problem – rather than the systematic application of rules of decoding. Barrs found that better readers began to combine the use of context with generalised phonic knowledge.

Substitutions reflect the use of three levels of language (see Chapter 3, page 43): Graphophonic, Syntactic and Semantic. They must therefore be coded separately, before transferring information to the main grid. Each substitution is considered from three aspects:

a) Is the response graphophonically similar to the original? It is usually sufficient to look at the matching of the first phoneme to determine this, although this is not completely fool-proof. It is in most cases quite obvious, however, if the child has been influenced by the look of the word to some extent.

b) Does the substitution fit grammatically into the sentence?

c) Does the substitution make sense within the whole passage – does it therefore fit semantically?

In the sample passage Angus made these substitutions:

	G|P	SYN	SEM
a	✗	✗	✗
b	✓	✓	✗
c	✗	✗	✗
d	✓	✓	✗
e	✓	✓	✗
f	✓	✓	✓
g	✗	✓	✓
h	✓	✓	✗
i	✓	✗	✗
j	✓	✓	✗

The two boys could see ~~nothing~~ *not*
insects which crept ~~between~~ his toes   *a*
Then the ~~laughing~~ *kept* turned into squeals   *b*
threads ~~from~~ *he* their bodies   *c*
Lie absolutely still *the*   *d*
darted ~~down~~ *obstinately* towards the boys *bodies*   *e*
had to duck to avoid *and*   *f*
the bird was ~~peeking~~ *pecking* at the threads *insects*   *g*
into the ground when they saw   *h*
the bird's ~~threatening~~ *then* beak *threading*   *i*
                                          j

A simple diagram to see how far the child is using all the available cueing systems records substitutions as members of overlapping sets, thus:

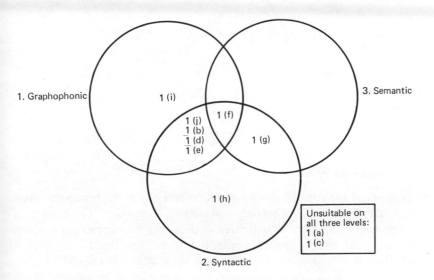

1. Graphophonic
1 (i)
1 (j)
1 (b)
1 (d)
1 (e)
1 (f)
1 (g)
3. Semantic
1 (h)
2. Syntactic

Unsuitable on all three levels:
1 (a)
1 (c)

This diagram is solely for demonstration of the method. Normally only the following diagram would be used.

The two miscues which do not fit into the circle show negative strategies. The 'best' substitutions occur in the shaded part of the diagram, showing close approximation to the original on all three language levels (in this case, only one comes in this category). Where the reader has used two out of the three levels with some success, we would still call these positive strategies (in this case, six). We can now transfer totals on to the original grid: six positive, four negative substitutions.

6. It is possible to infer from the evidence of even one reading some of the strategies which seem to be operating. A short case-study should be written to accompany the diagrammatic information, which, together with a tape reserved for the reader, would form the foundation of a satisfactory records system. (Of course it is advisable to start such recording in the early stages of reading, rather than beginning, as with this sample reader, at eight years old.)

ANGUS: SUBSTITUTION DIAGRAM (FINAL)

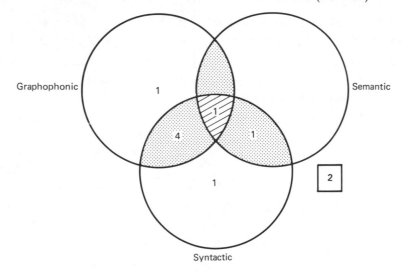

Notes on Angus

Angus read the passage slowly; he was apparently in the transition phase between Word by Word reading and Natural Intonation. The reading of the passage seemed to fall into three sections: the first (lines 1–9) was very hesitant, with both the refusals made in this section. About line 9, Angus was held up (probably by unexpected use of 'laughing' as a noun). He then became even more hesitant, and his reading faltered into Word by Word Rate. Lines 16–19 were read much faster, with hardly any hesitations and no repetitions. Here the substitutions were offered quickly and sometimes unreasoningly. Perhaps by this time Angus was anxious to get to the end of the task!

Hesitations were often made *after* the word which he found difficult, evidenced by a questioning inflection as he said it. Repetitions tended to be used more frequently, but *before* the word which was causing difficulty.

DIAGNOSING FROM THE GRID

The balance of fourteen positive to six negative miscues indicates a child who is well on the way to reading for understanding, but who does not have the skills of decoding as yet fully automised. He is beginning, though, to use context to hypothesise successfully, and his omissions and insertions show that he is also beginning to process the language of the text before re-encoding. The number of self-corrections are about average for a child of this reading age tackling a passage which is fairly difficult for him (readability level of passage was 9 years 4 months on Spache Readability Formula; Spache, 1953).

The substitution diagram supports the other evidence; only one in the 'target' area; not enough use of context cues, but full use of underlying syntactic knowledge. At the time when he read the passage, Angus was 8 years 2 months. His teacher classified him as an 'average' reader.

Recall of text

As suggested by Goodman (Chapter 3, page 47), we asked the reader for recall on the passage. In this case, Angus was asked to answer a set of multiple-choice questions. He scored twelve out of thirteen on factual, literal level questions and seven out of ten on inferential questions.

Examples of such questions and answers follow. The asterisk indicates the correct answer, and the initial 'A' the answers given by Angus.

Literal level
What colour was the prairie?
   Choices: Green
           Brown
           Yellow   * A

What happened when Mark's bare feet touched the ground?
    They started to itch   A
    Insects covered them   *
    They began to hurt
Where did Mark roll?
    Over and over on the ground   * A
    Under a bush
    Towards Thomas
Where did the insects go?
    Up a wall
    Into the ground   * A
    Across the prairie

Inferential

How do you know that nothing was growing on the prairie?
    The boys could see nothing but earth   *
    It was too hot
    The insects had eaten everything   A
How do you know that it was very hot?
    Mark took off some of his clothes   * A
    There was nothing to drink
    There were a lot of insects
Why did Mark begin to laugh?
    He was always giggling   A
    Thomas told him a joke
    The insects tickled him   *
Why did Mark's laughter turn to squeals?
    He was out of breath
    Thomas told him to stop laughing
    He was frightened   * A

Angus has been given as an example to demonstrate the method of analysis; it is, of course, more interesting when comparisons can be made, either with other readers or to detect developmental trends from the readings of one child. In the rest of the chapter we shall analyse a very young reader, and then compare in detail three reading transcripts of one older boy across a period of several months.

A YOUNG READER (Mary, 6+ years)

Mary read a story which, somewhat surprisingly, had a readability level of 8 years on the Spache formula. A transcript of her reading follows:

SOUP FOR DINNER

"I'll put four carrots in the big pot," said the old woman. "Four red carrots in the big pot." "Bubble, bubble, bubble," went the big pot, with one big jug of water, two good bones, three green cabbages, and four red carrots. Soup for dinner. Soup for all the children. "I'll put five potatoes in the big pot," said the old woman. "Five large round potatoes in the big pot." "Bubble, bubble, bubble," went the big pot, with one big jug of water, two good bones, three green cabbages, four red carrots and five large round potatoes. Soup for dinner. Soup for all the children. "Ah, the soup is ready," said the old woman, and she rang a bell. All the children came running in for dinner. All the children had a bowl of soup. All the children said, "This is lovely soup." Lovely soup made from one big jug of water, two good bones, three green cabbages, four red carrots and five large round potatoes.

(M. Hilton, unpublished MA thesis)

CODING

Type of miscue	Non-response	Substitution	Omission	Insertion	Reversal	Self correction	Totals
Positive	–	16	3	1	–	5	25
Negative	2	3	1	–	–	1	7

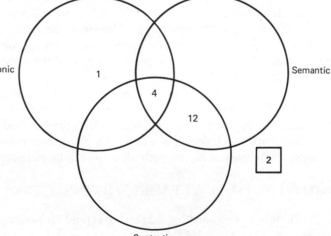

There are interesting comparisons to be made here with the evidence from Angus's reading. The balance of positive to negative miscueing for Mary is 25:7, indicating that she is reading 'for meaning'. Whereas Angus made miscues which were usually graphophonically suitable, most of Mary's lie in the syntactic/semantic dimensions. She exemplifies an earlier stage of reading, in that she is making guesses at what she thinks the text might contain, based partly on memory (this passage was half-way through a story) and partly on assumptions gained from experience *outside* the text.

It is necessary to take the text itself into consideration, as it must affect the strategies used. 'Soup for dinner' is a fairly typical example of an early reading text, containing much repetition and a clear rhythmical pattern. There is not much development of events; the situation of the old woman making soup is fairly predictable. The repetition of conventional adjectives (of colour, size, number) does not, however, make for the ease of reading which is presumably intended. Because the adjectives are often interchangeable there is no real incentive to use more than a modicum of hypothesising. In fact, when Mary deviates she often supplies phrases which are livelier in tone than the original, and which still manage to fit the story well, for example 'Hurray the porridge', 'All the children said "This is lovely"'.

So this six-year-old is using her 'everyday' language experience more than direct decoding skills (sound-symbol association), which she has probably only just begin to assimilate. The problem with children at this stage is to help them preserve this awareness of being able to use context, but to build up the ability to use more precise word-attack skills *at the same time*. What seems to happen far too often is that once a child becomes aware of phonics he is apt to use the graphophonic level to the exclusion of the other levels. It is probably inevitable that this imbalance will occur for a time with most children, but the myopia of within-word decoding sometimes persists for too long. This may be partly because of the oral reading demands made by the teacher, and partly because of the uneventful and stilted content of many early reading schemes.

These processes will be seen at work and will be looked at in more detail now, as we come to David, who was 8 years 8 months old at the time of his first reading, was diagnosed as a 'poor' reader by his teacher, had been seen by the educational psychologist, and had been given some remedial help. He read the same story as Angus, with whom he can be compared.

DAVID (READING 1): ATTACKED BY INSECTS

The great prairie was so wide that the two boys could see nothing but miles of yellow earth. "I feel like a grease-spot", said Mark, taking off his anorak.

(Handwritten miscues appear above the printed words; the reader's substitutions are noted in brackets.)

shoes [shaws] and socks [scores]. The minute [monster] his bare feet touched [took] the ground they were [there] covered by thousands of [their] tiny [time] insects [instead] which crept [kept] between [bet] his toes [test] and [a] tickled [take] him under his feet. He began [begged] to laugh [lag], and then found [fen] he [for] couldn't stop. He rolled over and over on the ground and the little insects [soon] covered him [comp] completely. One got into his ear [head] and he laughed [laid] even [every] more. Then the laughing [insects] turned [there] into [✓ scores] squeals [packs] of panic. The insects were pushing [pus] out little threads [threes] from [for] their bodies [bones] which fixed [Max] Mark [Might] to the ground. Soon [stood] he could not move [more], so tightly [thikt] was he pinned [pit] down. [Test] Thomas tried [them] to break [beak] the threads [threes], but they were as strong as nylon [nylwan]. "Lie [Little] absolutely [aspers] still", he ordered Mark [Mac], "and for goodness [goings] sake [sakes] stop yelling [yell / Singing]." Suddenly [bits] a bird flapped overhead [find / over] and darted [tossed] down towards [there] the boys. Thomas had to duck [under] to avoid [a / brid] the huge white [with / was] wings. Then he saw that the bird [a / brid / pracking and] was pecking at the [press / ther] threads to break them in two. The insects disappeared [deep surging] into the ground when they saw the bird's [boys] threatening beak. [break]

CODING

Type of miscue	Non-response	Substitution	Omission	Insertion	Reversal	Self correction	Totals
Positive	–	16	–	1	–	4	21
Negative	12	53	1	–	1	–	67

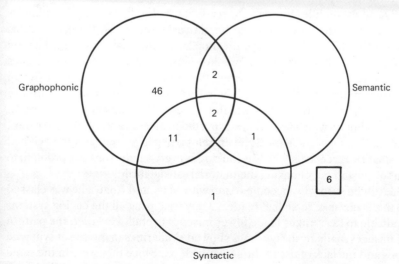

David read the passage very slowly, with every word separated, very much in the Word by Word stage. He also missed two or three full-stops, and was obviously unaware of juncture and stress – at least in reading this passage. He made frequent hesitations, immediately before the words causing difficulty. There were over forty hesitations, half of which occurred in the first paragraph, many more than his nine repetitions. The hesitations showed a poor eye-voice span, since they occurred immediately before the difficult word. The larger number of non-responses also mounted up in the first paragraph. David appeared, therefore, to be a reader greatly lacking in confidence, kept to a word by word pace partly because he was anxious not to make mistakes.

His four self-corrections were on small words which he knew; when he miscued badly on longer words, substituting items which often made no sense at all, he did not go back and self-correct.

David made very few insertions and omissions, usually, as has been shown, signs of a mature reader re-encoding the text in his own language. He did, though, make a great number of substitutions (a third of the total number of words in the passage). Only two of these were suitable on all three language levels; sixty-four evidenced an attempt to use the visual cueing system, and many of these illustrated the same type of strategy. David would sound the first phoneme of a word out loud (often correctly), and then repeat the sound in combination with the rest of the word. The rest of the word rarely continued to be graphophonically correct, and was even more rarely contextually suitable. He therefore knew that he should be matching sight with sound, but was unable to do this systematically beyond the first phoneme.

David exemplifies the stage in reading which follows Mary's; he knows his sounds up to a point, in isolation, thinks he should use them, but seems to lack the ability to bring syllabification and contextual guessing to bear on the problem. There is some hope, however, because many of his miscues were syntactically suitable, showing that he was using (unconsciously) an awareness of language structure. Nor were his substitutions often nonsense words – he had a vocabulary which he drew from whether it fitted or not: the vocabulary which he perhaps expected to meet in a story, like 'monster', 'instead', 'bones', 'singing'. Nevertheless, negative strategies outweighed positive by three to one; he was looking at every single word as a problem to be solved and not chunking the material satisfactorily.

It can be seen why, in comparison with Mary and Angus, he was classed at this stage as a 'remedial' reader. Mary was using all the cueing systems available to her; Angus made fewer miscues overall. However, the pattern of miscues made by the two boys showed similarities in the use of syntactic cues and the lack of use of the semantic level. Since they were in the same class, it could reflect the style of teaching reading. Without further evidence it would be unfair to make that assumption but a teacher could find much help from miscue analysis by surveying the errors made by a number of her class in this way. The passage, which was handled fairly easily by other children, soon showed itself as too difficult for David, which meant that his normal strategies might have been affected to some extent. This may account partly for his apparently great progress in three months (see *The Water Babies* on p. 74). This is one of the difficulties for a researcher dealing with unknown children; a teacher who knew her class would be able to provide a passage which taxed the reader without being frustrating. Nevertheless, David did manage to get to the end of the story and was able to answer many of the multiple-choice questions correctly, showing that even such a large number of miscues as he made does not necessarily indicate complete lack of understanding or involvement.

David was asked the same multiple-choice questions on the passage as Angus. He answered thirteen out of twenty-one correctly, a surprisingly good result considering his halting reading. How did he manage to get so many correct answers? Certainly not by blind guesswork; he varied his choice between the three possibilities, not always taking from the same position; he paused on some questions to think carefully before he answered. He must have utilised *all* the somewhat scanty evidence which he could have gleaned about the story. This can be seen by comparing his answers with his miscue analysis. For example, he answered the first question correctly – 'How many boys are there in the story?'. He had actually read 'two boys' himself. Similarly he got 'Where did the insects tickle Mark first?' correct, because he had read 'under his feet' correctly. Other questions were answered correctly because they involved words which had been supplied when David could not decode them; this seemed to indicate that there was nothing wrong with his memory or attention.

It is impossible to draw any firm conclusions about David's understanding of the passage, but it is clear that he was using a certain amount of reasoning. The overall impression of the reading and answering of questions was that the actual reading act had not yet become a 'real' experience for him. His acceptance of himself as a remedial reader may have added to his difficulties.

Five months later the school was revisited and David was asked, along with the other children, to read aloud again, this time from the book he was currently reading (an abridged version of *The Water Babies* (Spache Readability Level 9 years 3 months)). By now David was 9 years 1 month.

DAVID (READING 2)

The old lady looked at him, and then she said ~~out~~ at✓ loud, "He's sick, and I
~~cannot~~ can't ~~turn~~ try him away." And after she had ~~sent~~ set her little pupils away, she
gave Tom a cup of milk. "You'll sleep nice and/sound in my barn," she said,✓
and she laid Tom on the ~~soft~~ so✓, sweet hay and ~~put~~ put-pat✓ an old rug over him ~~until~~ sh—✓
she could make her plans to care for him. But Tom did not fall asleep.
Instead,✓ Inside her✓ ~~he~~ turned ~~and~~ a ~~tossed~~ toast✓ and he felt so hot all over that he|longed|to get
into the river and be cool. chime^
Then he heard the ~~sweet~~ swet sound of ~~church~~ chairs bells ringing, and all of a
sudden he found himself in the ~~middle~~ mild✓ of a meadow with the stream just
before him.

The Waterbabies

CODING: DAVID (2)

Type of miscue	Non-response	Substitution	Omission	Insertion	Reversal	Self correction	Totals
Positive	–	5	–	–	–	6	11
Negative	1	8	–	1	–	2	12

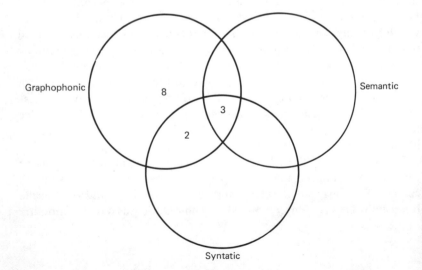

David's reading had changed completely in style. He read the passage very fast, though still ignoring some of the sentence junctures. He made only one non-response, and few hesitations. His repetitions were now made to reassure himself on words which had puzzled him, and he often repeated his self-corrections as a self-checking device. The increase in the number of self-corrections gives a crucial indication of the new pattern in his reading. He wanted the story to make sense; it is important, though, to remember that self-corrections demonstrate an interim stage in reading development, since a mature reader is unlikely to use them. David was still anxious to be accurate – two of his self-corrections were unnecessary. In one case he actually said the right word 'put' and micorrected it to 'pat'. Median vowels were still giving him trouble, and it worried him if he could not recognise them.

The pattern of his substitutions shows similar conflict between his desire to get meaning and the right phonic response. He still, therefore, made more substitutions which were graphophonically appropriate but contextually unsuitable, many of which he self-corrected. The example of 'chime' instead of 'church' bells (first response 'chairs') shows his overall strategy well. He tended, as in his first reading, to match his initial response to the first phoneme, without much thought, but now he did not let that pass. He went back and corrected himself, bringing in the use of context slightly later than his attempt to sound out the word. So his negative strategies were reduced greatly in relation to the positive.

There were no set questions on this passage, and David was asked to say in his own words as much as he could remember of the story, (which was some way into the story book which he had already read.)

Transcript of recall on *The Waterbabies*

D.   Well, Tom didn't feel very well, so the lady thought, 'Shall I turn him out or keep him and look after him?' So she put a rug over him, she said 'Go to sleep and stay', and then – but he didn't go to sleep.

Questioner: Why didn't he go to sleep?

D.   Because he was lost.

Q.   And what did he wish he could do?

D.   Go and get into the river.

Q.   And then what?

D.   He was in the middle of the meadow with a stream running over him.

Q.   Yes. Was he really in the middle of the meadow?

D.   No. He was just dreaming.

David remembered not only most of the events of what he had just read in sequence (he also added a summary of what had gone on before), but, more importantly, and quite startlingly, he transformed the language of the original text into his own and collected some of the smaller incidents together in condensed form. Not only that, but he was aware of the deeper level of meaning which was not obvious from a literal reading. Although no actual mention was made in the text of Tom falling asleep, David realised that the last paragraph was the precursor to a dream sequence, vital to understanding of the whole book.

David seemed to have made so much progress that he was immediately given another page to read from a book picked out at random from the teacher's bookshelf, in an attempt to see how he tackled informational text. This was not used purely for diagnosis; the teacher helped David where necessary, so the situation became instructional. The transcript of the interaction follows, without miscue analysis. It can be seen that David used the same sort of strategies, however, as he had done in reading the story. He made several attempts on single words rather than letting his first miscue pass. The asterisks on the coded passage show where help was given. The transcript of the interview shows how quickly David responded to clues suggested on all three language levels.

DAVID (READING 3):

WHAT CAUSES VOLCANOES? (SPACHE READABILITY LEVEL 9 YEARS 3 MONTHS)

A volcano is an | opening in the earth's crust. It is an | opening where gas and rock come from inside the earth on to the surface. The rock is usually very hot – so hot that it is MOLTEN, which means "melted".
* Scientists call this molten rock MAGMA. It is a special kind of rock. It contains crystals of minerals. Usually the crystals are dissolved in the hot magma, somewhat as salt or sugar dissolves in hot water.

What causes Volcanoes? Transcript of Interaction
David (reading): A volcano is an / ope-ing opening in the earth's cracks. It is an / opening where gas and rock come from inside the earth on to the sur / face. The rock is / usually very hot so hot that it is m-o-lten / molten / which means / molted.
Teacher. Not quite molted.
D. M-E-

T.	Melted – Right.
D.	Scin -
T.	Oh, that's a hard one, isn't it? Who are the people who talk about rock and do a lot of experiments?
D.	Scientists.
T.	Good boy, yes.
D.	can-call this me-
T.	This was the one you had up there.
D.	Call this / molten rock mag-a
T.	Magma
D.	Magma – magma. Is-it is a spocal king of rock.
T.	Now wait a minute. What's that word?
D.	k - i - d / kid
T.	No. You know that word. It's an easy one.
D.	Ki-
T.	It is a –
D.	king / k-i-g
T.	Kind of rock. Now what's that word?
D.	Special
T.	Special kind of rock. Good.
D.	contents / cracks / crumbles
T.	No. Crystals
D.	of m -
T.	Can you sound that one out?
D.	Min -
T.	Yes. Min -
D.	-er
T.	-als
D.	Minerals. Minerals, usually the cra-
T.	Crystals
D.	Crystals are droven – droved – drift
T.	What does that say?
D.	Dis -
T.	Now what does this?
D.	slove
T.	-solved
D.	Dissolved in the hot magma, some / somewhat as s-alt / sort or sug-
T.	Look along and then you might guess what those are. What's that one? You've had that. You did that. What's the beginning there?
D.	/ di – dislov
T.	Dissolves
D.	In hot water.

The transcript shows how the teacher's help focuses the child on a particular level of language (this will be discussed more fully in the next chapter), which may or may not be the most helpful in reality for the child. His pick-up of contextual cueing (for example, jumping to the word 'scientist') seems much quicker and more adept than his struggles to 'sound out' words. His undoubted progress across the few months since his first reading must have come mainly from his realisation that he could and should use context cues, to compensate for what is probably a poor auditory memory. He had no special help between the first and last readings. His teacher reported that the remedial advisory teacher had stopped coaching him, and that she herself coped with him as well as she could in a small village school with a mixed-age class. His case illustrates clearly the capability of children to make progress without much direct individual instruction.

The discussion on content which followed the reading demonstrates the strong motivation which David seemed to possess to understand what he read. It also demonstrates how perseverance is necessary on the part of the teacher, since at one point it would have been only too easy to accept David's feeling (unfounded) that he had understood nothing.

Transcript of discussion on 'volcanoes' (Text available)

T. Now just stop because it's very difficult. You have to be a scientist to do this. Let's just work out what it's about. It says that a volcano is a what?

D. Opening.

T. An opening. So what does it look like then, a volcano?

D. A kind of – (demonstrating with hands) – it goes along and then comes up like that – and a big hole in the middle.

T. That's right. So that it's really – what's happened to make that hole? It's the –

D. The earth had come out.

T. That's right. The earth's crust has cracked open, and then, what comes from inside that?

D. Gas and that.

T. Good. That's gas. That's right. And worse than gas, what else?

D. Rock.

T. Great lumps of stone. So it's not very nice to be – Now what is there special about the rock? Does it tell you? What's different about the rock that it throws up?

D. It's a special kind.

T. Yeah, but something about it. Would you like to touch it?

D. No, it's very hot.

T. It's very hot. It's so that that it's –

D. Melted.

T. That's right. Now imagine rock being melted. Why is it so hot, do you think?

D. Is it because of the gas and that?

T. Yes, where does it come from?

D. The ground.

T. That's right. So what is it like in the ground?

D. Hot.

T. There must be a big fire inside. So all that rock's come from miles down and it's all hot. And what do they call it, the scientists, that rock? They give it a special name.

D. Magma.

T. That's right. Magma. And in it, it's got little crystals. Do you know what crystals are?

D. It's kind of glass.

T. They look like glass, and the crystals have been dissolved in the rock, like you dissolve sugar in water. You've seen sugar and salt dissolve in hot water, haven't you? Because it's so hot the crystals dissolve . . . Do you understand that?

D. (Shakes head)

T. What bit don't you understand? Because you've read it all right. What's the bit you don't get?

D. Don't know.

T. None of it? But you *do* know. Now you know what a volcano is, don't you?

D. Mm.

T. You know what comes out of the volcano?

D. Mm.

T. What?

D. Hot rock.

T. Can you imagine that in your mind?

D. It would be all runny.

T. What?

D. It would be all runny.

T. That's *right*! It's all runny, and inside that hot rock there are little–

D. Crystals.

T. Crystals! And they're dissolved into the rock, because it's so hot. Now what is there you don't understand about that?

D. Nothing.

T. You understand it all, so why did you say you didn't?

D. I didn't at first.

It seemed worthwhile to report the conversation verbatim, not as a model to follow, but to show how the overall grasp of meaning gradually developed. By reading it first, not entirely satisfactorily, then by clarifying certain individual concepts, the child was getting hold of isolated ideas, but had not put them together into a conceptual frame-work. When he volunteered information of his own accord, the tone of his voice and the expression on his face implied that at last it had 'clicked', and then all the individual items made more sense for him. Until we can spend some time talking to children in this way, reading skills may be mastered, facts may be churned back as 'comprehension exercises', but the dawn of realisation may never break. Until this happens, it is likely that a child will not understand the true function of reading.

It is hoped that in describing the diagnostic procedure with a small selection of readers, in detail, we have helped teachers to see the point of using some such measures in their classrooms.

Chapter 5 will describe how the practice of reading aloud can be used positively and constructively in teaching. It will be emphasised that it can be used as a means of interaction between teacher and pupil, and as a communicative activity for groups of children. Some practical suggestions for classroom organisation and adaptation will follow in Chapter 6.

5 Learning through reading aloud

Much emphasis has been laid on the value of the diagnosis of reading strategies from listening to children reading aloud. The purpose of diagnosis, however, is to form a valid basis for action, and the next chapters will move to examining the activity in the context of the whole language curriculum. Doubt has been cast on the value of the practice as it is so often carried out in classrooms; this does not mean that it can serve no useful purpose, or that it need be considered merely a ritual, to be replaced entirely by silent reading. It would be useful for a teacher to survey the reading activities of her class wherever they occur, and to ensure the right balance between oral and silent reading. Hearing children read is neither more nor less important than reading to children or discussing the content of what has been read; all are part of the same objective – to encourage a child to read independently for many different purposes. The main emphasis is on cognitive learning; hearing reading is not mainly for social interaction or for maintaining the individual contact with a child as a method of 'individualised teaching'. Its purpose should be to show children how to use all the cueing systems available to them through positive reinforcement.

The practicability of the activity should be evaluated objectively.

The recommendation to hear children read as often as possible, for example 'Once a child has started upon a reading scheme the aim should be to hear him read a little every day' (Moyle, 1968) is considered by Campbell (1981) to be 'based on subjective "armchair" perceptions of the interaction'. Where researchers have observed the practice happening in schools (Campbell, 1981; Southgate *et al.*, 1981; Maxwell, 1977) they have invariably discovered that the time allocation given to any child exclusively is minimal. The 'Extending Beginning Reading' Research team (Southgate *et al.*, 1981) found that hearing reading was rarely used instructionally; the main purpose seemed to be as a regular check on quantity. When a child failed to recognise a word, he was usually prompted immediately, and there was rarely any discussion of decoding difficulties, or of content. It might be more profitable if oral reading individually to the teacher was carried out far less frequently, but with more positive objectives.

Miscue analysis, which has already been described in detail, is likely to change the teacher's attitude to her task. When she realises that reading is a problem–solving activity which is closely linked to the child's overall language experience, she will look on herself less as an instructor than as one who shares in the child's reading, encouraging him to use the strategies which are most suitable for him and for the particular text. She will also organise the classroom so that children may share their reading with each other.

Reading will become part of the general language interaction between pupil and teacher and pupil and pupil. In listening to the child read, the teacher will help him to realise what cues are offered by the language. This interaction at its best will be between teacher, pupil *and text*, in that responses to the text can be shared and analysed, and different layers of meaning investigated. It can show, even in the earliest stages, that the written word is not just to be remembered as literal fact, but can be evaluated in terms of 'true' or 'false', 'good' or 'bad' writing. Through the interaction the teacher can draw on the added dimension of the child's own experiences outside, but connected with, the text. She will realise that great interest in a particular story or theme can overcome difficulties in decoding. In other words, such a 'shared reading activity' will be a valuable and important occasion, which may only happen once a fortnight instead of once a day, because it would be impracticable to carry out such sessions more frequently.

Above all, the shared 'interview' would try to develop independent 'attack' in the reader as soon as possible. Children would be encouraged to become aware of their own strategies, including the encouragement to use contextual hypothesising. Most children do not ever admit that they 'guess' a word, or miss a word out, evidently thinking that these are faulty tactics. It is this *attitude* rather than a skill which is to be developed: a willingness to look ahead, to use all the resources of language available. Children must not rely on the folk-myths surrounding learning to read, such as the idea that they should 'sound out' a word letter by letter because that is expected of them. Phonic skills are important, but only as part of the whole reading task.

We are therefore thinking of a 'shared reading interview' where the teacher would be consciously suggesting ways of using all three levels of reading. It would not involve merely hearing the child read, and indeed could vary considerably in content from one occasion to another. The following ingredients could make up the total recipe:

Teacher reads some of the text.
Child reads some of the text.
Teacher sets a purpose at beginning of interview to encourage skimming and scanning to find certain elements in text.

Teacher asks child to read a paragraph silently first and then to read it aloud.

Teacher asks child to read a paragraph silently and then questions him on it.

Teacher encourages child to ask questions about text that has just been read (either by himself or teacher).

Teacher discusses decoding problems with child (having carried out miscue analysis in advance).

Teacher and child discuss contents of text in terms of appreciative/ emotional response.

Teacher discusses child's difficulties in reading in general, attitudes, likes and dislikes and so on, (see interview format at end of Chapter 3).

The ingredients would vary from reading to reading, and would very much depend on the text that had been chosen. As soon as possible books outside a reading scheme should be included.

It is clear that such an approach involves a greater emphasis on the content of reading. The session would become a relaxed, and, it is hoped, enthusiastic dialogue between teacher and pupil. Inevitably, this type of interview would lead to the development of intermediate and higher order skills, the awareness of reading as a skill which involves both decoding and the use of context cues. He would also begin to appreciate the different levels of interpretation which can operate in understanding text fully. The child could be sent away with specific problems to investigate, short-term goals set in advance for his private reading. These would often encourage quick scanning of a whole paragraph rather than word-by-word reading. The individual contact would not disappear, but its emphasis would change, and there should be a growing awareness on the reader's part of the function rather than the techniques of reading.

To propose such complex interaction seems perhaps over-idealistic; the teacher would need to know the text to some extent, and would need to concentrate on one child exclusively, without the constant interruptions which seem to occur in most classrooms. The corollary is twofold; perhaps the individual reading interviews would have to be shared with other children who are at the same stage of development on some occasions. This would mean a return to *group* reading. The second implication is that the rest of the class must be trained to work independently without constant need of help – again, this may mean children working together to achieve purposeful goals. The problem of organisation is far from easy to solve, and will be discussed in Chapter 6.

It is impossible to list in detail all the possible ways in which a teacher might utilise the reading interview. Some of them have been touched on in earlier chapters, and most are accepted practice in many schools. The ways in which the child is helped directly in word-recognition skills, however, warrants further attention. Until recently there has been little research on what actually happens when such instruction is being given to individual children, but two studies have been published recently which should be of direct practical interest.

John Gulliver's paper, 'Teachers' Assumptions in Listening to Reading' (Gulliver, 1979), shows how he set out to observe how far teachers reflected, consciously or unconsciously, their assumptions about the nature of reading when they were hearing their pupils read. He observed the interactions in progress by tape-recording six experienced and successful teachers, mainly in infant schools, carrying out this practice with children of varying ability, 'under normal pressures'. Transcriptions of the tapes included the original text, the child's responses, and any interchange which took place between pupil and teacher.

The terms used in reporting the events were derived from Sinclair and Coulthard's analysis of discourse (1975), classified into 'moves' made by teachers and the 'exchanges' which often followed. Gulliver, in concentrating on the teachers' moves, attempted to classify the underlying purpose determining them. He found 'no less than 53 distinguishable types of move' used in 41 lessons, revealing the complexity behind what may appear superficially a simple activity. He then subsumed these 53 moves into 10 main functions.

'It was felt that the ten general functions could themselves be classified according to whether they were mainly influenced by views of reading process or of learning, and by whether the pupil's role was primarily active or passive.' The functions ranged from *conditioning*, when the teacher quickly corrected any error, and reinforced the child with praise if he repeated the correction successfully, to moves which carried the conversation *beyond the immediate reading* to encourage the child to bring his own critical awareness to the problem. An example is given (Gulliver, p. 47):

ELICITING CRITICISM

Original text

*Now we'll have to stop talking
and join the huddle of penguins,
because the wind is getting up
and it will be very cold soon.*

> 1 Pupil – is that what they're
> called/together/a huddle/

At this point the teacher could have simply answered 'yes' and asked the pupil to continue. But she didn't:

> 2 Teacher – that's right/yes/
> yes/think it's rather a good
> name/a huddle of penguins/
> don't you?
> 3 P. – Yes
> 4 T. – because you do huddle
> up together sometimes/don't
> you/ to keep warm
> 5 P. – yes/you get in a huddle.

Gulliver comments on that fact that this exchange is initiated by the pupil and is therefore likely to have more 'cognitive clarity'; the exchange is directly comparable with David's spontaneous contribution 'It would be all runny', described in Chapter 4.

The categories may be broadly divided according to whether they encourage a tentative, reflective approach to reading, giving the child opportunity to hypothesise from the context, or whether they encourage concentration on the graphic information, demanding accurate decoding, in which case the teacher may use the occasion to remind the pupil of phonic rules, or may intervene swiftly if a mistake is made. For example (p. 50):

ATTENDING TO GRAPHIC INFORMATION

Original Text

Simon and Elizabeth
1 (Pupil) Simon and Elizabeth
are playing with the clay.
2 P. are playing with the clay.
They have got it out of the bin.
3 P. They have got it out of the
(hesitates)

4 P. – what's that word?
5 (Teacher) – you can sound that one
6 P. – pin
7 T. – yes/but put the right letter in front/what is that/a . . . (pointing to the first letter of *bin*)
8 P. – pun
9 T. – that's . . . (last two letters of *bin*)
10 P. – in
11 T. – and that's . . .
12 P. pin
13 T. – no/that's not a 'p' is it/it's a . . .

At this point another pupil provided the word which was required and the problem was resolved.

Gulliver suggests that here the teacher is viewing reading as a passive process of decoding graphic symbols to sounds.

The following categories (described in detail in his paper) were isolated as teachers' *moves*:

1 Establishing literal meaning
2 Encouraging inference
3 Eliciting criticism
4 Emphasising tentativeness
5 Explaining
6 Providing conditions for induction
7 Attending to meaning and language
8 Attending to graphic information
9 Demanding accurate re-coding
10 Conditioning

Obviously the teacher's style of correction is going to influence the child's approach to reading much more than either may realise. Gulliver was interested in finding out how consistent teachers were in selecting certain types of move. He used both formal analysis and 'impressionistic' report to draw his conclusions. He found (admitting his limited sample) a remarkable consistency in individual teachers' moves. Where some would see errors as mistakes in decoding, others would judge similar errors as a 'failure to perceive meaning'; and would probe, sometimes at length, to allow the child to work out the implications of the text. He suggests that the teachers' assumptions remained the same 'regardless of differences in pupils and differences in text'.

Admittedly Gulliver is biased towards Goodman's view of reading as a 'psycholinguistic guessing game'. It would be inadvisable to suggest a distortion of strategies so that no attention is given to graphic cues, or to make each move so lengthy that the thread of the narrative is lost. However, the research is very useful for teachers as a mirror to observe their own practices. Gulliver rightly points out that children are very quick to adapt their ways of working to what they believe the teacher requires. Perhaps this is the lesson they learn most successfully in school!

The *Extending Beginning Reading* interviews (op. cit., p. 58) showed that most 7–9 year olds believed that it was 'wrong' to guess a word they did not know, or to leave it out and go on to the next word. It is unlikely that they have actually been told this; it is much more probable that they have deduced such attitudes because they were never told positively of the variety of cueing systems available. As Gulliver asks, 'How far does the capacity of a child to become an active interrogator of the text have its roots in the interaction between teacher and pupil in the early stages of reading acquisition?'

Another study on similar lines is reported in the *Journal of Research in Reading* (Campbell, 1981). Campbell observed six teachers in infant classrooms, and reported their interactions during 'hearing children read' activities. He found frequent attention switching from the child reading to attend to other children (as did the 'Extending Beginning Reading' project). He categorised what he saw differently from Gulliver, and divided the 'pedagogical moves' into:

1 Emphasising the one-to-one relationship of the encounter, the teacher's awareness of the individual problems of a particular child
2 Giving directions which indicate a way of procedure
3 Providing words
4 Encouraging the child to recognise the miscued word
5 Directing phonic analysis
6 Asking comprehension questions, either about individual words or the whole passage read

The frequencies of these moves when averaged among the six teachers showed a fair balance between all six categories. Individual teachers however varied very much in the average number of moves made during a session (that is in the number of 'teaching points') and in the distribution between the categories.

Both researchers suggest that their systems could be adapted by teachers to observe their own practices in listening to children read. This would be impossible, of course, without tape-recording the sessions and then analysing their tactics. Usually, the balance between swift prompting, correction and encouraging the use of context and meaning, will vary according to the needs of different pupils. We can see a direct continuum between miscue analysis and the adoption of particular teaching strategies.

In summing up the tactics available to the teacher when a problem occurs in the child's reading, it is likely that the one or more of the following ploys will be used:

a. Supplying the word
b. Asking for words to be sounded out
c. Asking what the first letter of the word 'says'
d. Covering part of word up and encouraging syllabification
e. Stopping child if word is said wrongly and asking for correct response
f. Asking child to guess from what has gone before
g. Asking child to look ahead and then guess what word might be
h. Letting child proceed without correction
i. Waiting for child to think

Many of these tactics involve concentration on the word alone. Don Holdaway, in his useful book *The Foundations of Literacy* (1979) emphasises how important it is to use 'integration strategies' which 'put the parts together again' and remind the reader that word-recognition is only a step on the way to understanding the whole text. He pinpoints the strategies which do this most successfully, and shows that children will often develop such strategies unconsciously. It is the ones who do not develop such independence who must be directed towards them:

The re-run: Looking back on previous words and paragraphs to get the 'drift' of the text. Becomes less necessary as short-term memory develops.
Read-on: Looking at rest of sentence to solve problem. Cloze procedure (word deletion exercises) may be a helpful device for encouraging this.
Picture: 'A scrutiny of illustrations in the light of the developing sentence may provide the elusive cue'. Personal imagery should replace actual pictures as reading develops.
Identification: 'I have seen that word somewhere before' feeling. Exploitation of children's accurate visual memories of when they have met it previously.
Comparison: Comparison with a more familiar word which has similar elements. This may involve prefixes, suffixes, familiar vowel digraphs

and so on. Again, may involve associations with other words which are largely subconscious.

Pumfrey (1977, pp. 164–5) gives some guidance on teaching the use of context cues. He emphasises that the more complex the sentence, the more difficult it is to use context successfully. 'A knowledge of the pupil's interests and background experience is helpful.' The type of questions used will elicit different strategies; for example questions beginning with 'who, which, what, why and how' produce definite information, whereas questions like 'Can you think of a word for that space?' are too vague to be of much help. Questions like 'How did you know that it was that word?' or 'Which word helped you to decide?' help the reader to 'become aware of how he is using context' and the teacher to find out what use the child is making of it. The realisation that the meaning of words with multiple interpretations and different pronunciations (for example, minute, wind) 'is in fact determined by their context might be reached intuitively by the child. More probably, he will need to be taught this' (op. cit. p. 166).

As the brief of this book is to consider *Listening to Children Reading*, the shared interview between teacher and child has been given prime importance. However, reading aloud does, or should, occur in other classroom situations, and brief mention will be made of these no less important opportunities for 'sharing text'.

Before the advent of the tape-recorder, children reading aloud to themselves would have been thought of as in a transitory phase, to be passed through as quickly as possible. The monitoring advantages of the tape-recorder have probably not been exploited as much as they might have been. The BBC 'Listen and Read' programmes indicate one very valuable use, particularly for children who find it difficult to get beyond the word-by-word stage. Tapes of stories (commercial or made by the teacher) are made available for the reader to listen to while he follows in the text. It is important that the taped reading should be as lively and fluent as possible. When he feels ready, the child can then read the same passage into the tape-recorder himself, checking back on both readings to see how far he has succeeded. When convenient, the teacher may listen to the child's reading with him, and help him to survey his strategies and to devise alternatives.

Carol Chomsky (Chomsky, 1976) describes in great detail a variation on this approach, which was carried out with eight-year-old backward readers. Children were helped to choose books of twenty to thirty pages which would be a little too difficult for them and to listen to a tape-recorded reading while following in the text until they felt ready to read part of the book themselves. Although it took some of the children a month to read a whole book fluently, they became very enthusiastic, and were encouraged to take the books and tapes home if they liked. Apparently what began as memorisation of the tape gradually became 'real reading'. This was supported by numerous language games related directly to the stories in use, and the article described these in detail. For instance, the child might select the words he found difficult in several pages of text; these would be put on cards and kept as an individual bank for learning. The teacher might ask the child to find a certain word quickly on the page, or alternatively the child would pick out a word for the teacher to find. Wooden letters were used to build up words within the text. All these language-games are in common use; the interesting variant here is that they were linked directly with a continuous text which the pupil was attempting to internalise by more global methods. Carol Chomsky found that progress was impressive with all the children concerned: she believed that they were learning to 'shift their focus from the individual word to connected discourse and to integrate their fragmented knowledge'.

In many classrooms there seem to be two distinct modes of reading, which exist as discrete activities for children. The first we have described at length: the public competitive practice of reading aloud individually to the teacher. The second is the private practice of reading silently, which some pupils may not enjoy, particularly since it seems alien to the gregariousness of many seven to ten-year-olds. The 'sharing' of reading which it has been suggested should be the underlying impetus of the interaction between teacher and individual child, might be extended to 'sharing' of reading between children. Reading aloud then serves a different function, not an instructional activity, but as a means of communication for shared enjoyment. Many group activities which use reading as a focus have been suggested recently (see, for example Walker, 1974; Lunzer and Gardner, 1979). Some of these activities will be listed in the next chapter, since they depend on particular kinds of organisation. Here we are stating the importance of the principle; reading aloud for 'sharing' is an act which has to be trained and developed. Young children will rarely be able to read well 'unseen', so that silent reading as preparation for performance will be necessary.

Such reading aloud can be a way of enhancing personal appreciation and understanding of a story, play or poem through its communication to others, a skill which has been an important element in all cultures from minstrels, balladeers and town-criers to actors and preachers.

The aim will be to develop in children an acceptance of oral reading as a conscious act, in which the reader becomes the author's 'instrument'. Some children may never become great practitioners, but most will gain confidence from the activity and will learn how to please, move and persuade an audience of their own age, and how to listen appreciatively to others.

The reading matter must be carefully chosen for this purpose. In poetry, rhythms must be strong, and vocabulary evocative. In reading aloud, children learn to enjoy the sound and feel of highly alliterative onomatopœic phrases 'rolling round their tongues'. They will learn to put colour into their voices by slightly heightened use of intonation and pause. They will realise how the 'double layers' of meaning can be conveyed by flexible tone or paralinguistic features (like the raising of an eyebrow). If they are lucky they will already have found a good model in the teacher reading to them. They may begin in their private reading to look for extracts which will appeal to listeners. A half-hour of self-selected passages from stories which are chosen, for instance, for their excitement, or their fun, or their sadness, will help young readers to be aware of style and mood.

With young children audience participation is the beginning of such sensitivity. The repetitions of nursery rhymes and fairy stories invite others to join in, as do the choruses of ballads. While a child is still learning to read it is useless to tell him to 'put expression' into his reading, but later it is possible to show him the techniques of voice production and dramatic reading. All sorts of material besides conventional stories and poetry can feed this awareness; the joke books which are such favourites with children of nine to eleven can be exploited. How do you read a joke well? How do you deliver the punch-line? What is different about reading a 'shaggy dog' story from a limerick? Similarly, advertisements are a rich source, and children who imitate television advertisements perfectly could transfer their skill to making up and reading aloud their own creations.

A development has been suggested in this chapter from reading aloud individually to the teacher as a way of gaining confidence and word-recognition skills, to reading aloud as a communicative activity. It is important, of course, that silent reading should develop in parallel, and that the public occasions of reading aloud should be preceded by a preparation time of silent reading before the presentation. The tape-recorder is a valuable adjunct, particularly for shy readers, who may prefer to present their reading as a disembodied voice, which can be 'tried out' and re-recorded before it reaches their friends' critical ears.

6 The organisation of reading aloud

In earlier chapters we have questioned the amount of time given to listening to individual children read, and raised doubts as to whether it is possible to use this as a valid instructional procedure in classes of thirty. This chapter will suggest ways in which teachers can plan across the curriculum in order to give practice and help in developing efficient reading, bearing in mind both the needs of individuals and the problem of numbers. This can only be achieved by a teacher consciously working out the most economical use of her own time – the most precious commodity – and deciding how she can train her pupils to carry out self-evaluation and become independent, responsible learners. On occasion she must listen to individuals reading and discuss their work with them; this means that work must be provided for the rest of the class which is carefully paced with in-built self-checking devices. It is important that reading should not be considered as an isolated technique to be covered only at certain times of the day. All subject areas provide fruitful opportunities for reading, both silently and aloud, and it is therefore unnecessary to provide times for 'comprehension', 'phonic drills' and so on except for short initiatory periods. There must be, however, a clear assessment and recording policy, so that a child's development in reading can be checked quickly by any interested party (teacher, head-teacher, adviser and others). Many teachers who run well-organised classes realise that the great amount of time needed for initial planning will be amply repaid by the purposefulness of even very young children working within a secure structure.

THE INDIVIDUAL READING INTERVIEW AND RECORD-KEEPING

This has been described in detail in Chapter 5, but the teacher will have to decide how often and with whom it is carried out, and how she will record the results. Many teachers try to hear every child read as often as possible. The value of this should be considered very seriously. Children are not going to change their reading strategies overnight, and it is impossible, even with frequent sessions, to do more than sample their mastery of vocabulary and their ability to make sense of what they read; in any case they may perhaps be better assessed by other means (group discussion and observation of writing development, for instance). If miscue analysis is to be employed, it is suggested that on taking over a class, a teacher should hear as many children as possible read (the tape-recordings can be analysed gradually out of the classroom). The teacher can gain from this initial hearing an idea of the spread of development across the class; she can isolate the efficient readers, who can then be given silent reading programmes, and those at risk, who will need more frequent individual interviews. She will be able at this point to select about six different passages for duplication, which will cover the span of reading levels in the class. They will be stored ready for presentation to individuals at suitable intervals throughout the term. As we have shown, even one reading can afford a great deal of information when analysed, so it is not envisaged that any child would need more than three diagnostic sessions a term. One of these could well be a self-recording. Older children could read a passage into the recorder, and play it back to themselves while following the text. They might then tape-record their impressions of their own reading. This would be interesting in the light it might throw on children's attitudes to what 'good' reading involves.

If the duplication of texts is difficult, an acetate sheet may be placed over the page for coding purposes.

For additional information on the child's use of context cues, a selection of difficult words taken from the passage may be printed on separate cards. The child is asked to read these before he is given the passage. Surveying the words read correctly, first in isolation and then in context will show how far he is making use of the content level.

It could be useful to collect a series of substitution 'diagrams' (See Chapter 4, page 65) on one sheet of paper, with short comments and prescriptive notes. (At least one teacher has found this useful.) For an example see overleaf, p. 94.

The page would usually be devoted to one child's reading, although a variation would be to complete a sheet with substitution records of different children in the class. Time might reveal to a teacher that she may be employing an unbalanced instructional programme.

The case-studies in Chapter 4 illustrated certain stages of development in reading. Individual analyses should always be considered in the light of 'normal' patterns of development. Donald's list of stages (Donald, 1980) may be useful as guidelines here:

EXAMPLE: RECORDING SUBSTITUTIONS

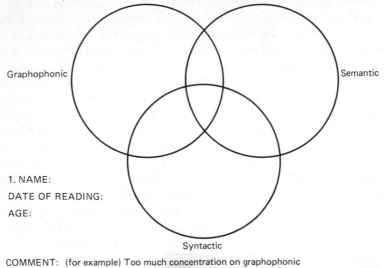

1. NAME:
DATE OF READING:
AGE:

COMMENT: (for example) Too much concentration on graphophonic
level. Good use of syntax. Help needed in guessing from
context. Give cloze procedure exercise.

Developmental sequence of strategies

1. *Early stage*

Miscues show child responding with words or phrases which he has probably met in earlier reading. Child is therefore expecting familiar patterns to emerge, but is not yet aware that new combinations of letters and words are likely to be introduced, or that reading matter will continually provide new information (exemplified by Mary's reading, Chapter 4, page 69ff).

2. Child uses contextual cues, especially syntactic, before graphophonic cueing system is readily available; few miscues are related graphically to the stimulus word in the text. Use of context is 'loose' and non-generalised. (See Mary as above.)

3. *No-response stage*

Uncertainty. Growing awareness of graphic constraints, but inability to integrate them with proper use of context, leading to conflict situation (exemplified by David's first reading, Chapter 4, pages 70–1).

4. Ability to use all cueing systems simultaneously, leading to integrated use of contextual and graphic constrains (exemplified by David's second reading, Chapter 4, page 74).

Although it is helpful to review the individual child's reading within the sort of broad developmental framework suggested above, it must be emphasised that diagnosis through miscue analysis can never be norm-referenced in the same way as standardised reading tests. The teacher may find it useful, though, to compare her diagnosis with reading ages. It may then be seen how children with the same reading age are often using very different strategies and are therefore at different stages of competence.

In *Reading After Ten*, (Goodacre *et al.* 1977, page 78), Christopher Walker suggests that it is sometimes useful to record class trends in oral reading progress, which would, of course, be an amalgam of individual record sheets. His itemised headings are reproduced here:

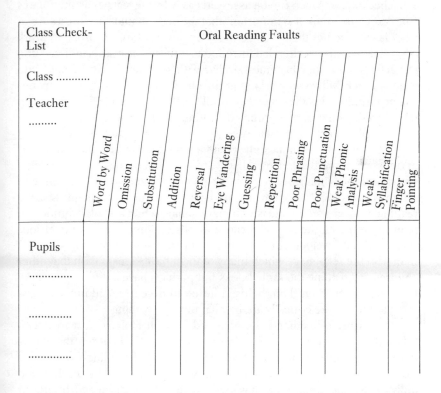

Class Check-List	Oral Reading Faults												
Class .... Teacher	Word by Word	Omission	Substitution	Addition	Reversal	Eye Wandering	Guessing	Repetition	Poor Phrasing	Poor Punctuation	Weak Phonic Analysis	Weak Syllabification	Finger Pointing
Pupils													

It is noticeable that Walker's list indicates a difference in attitude from that suggested by miscue analysis, in that he labels all deviations from the original as 'faults' to be noted for remediation. It is suggested that the format could be adapted by replacing the word 'fault' by 'miscue', and by using plus and minus signs in the grid to record the use of positive and negative strategies. These would have to indicate a general trend towards 'positive' or 'negative' since the grid for a class could not contain the detailed information of an individual analysis.

ORGANISING GROUPS

It may be more economical to group children at times for oral reading. By 'groups' we do not envisage children reading in unison, which was probably what discredited 'group reading' originally. It is the type of organisation used least in classrooms, understandably, since it is the most difficult to organise satisfactorily. Teachers are loath to abandon the direct instructional role, and feel that children may waste time if left to work together. The only antidote to this is to set short-term goals for groups, which are self-checking, or which can be assessed easily by the teacher as she rotates from group to group. It is important that the class should be made aware of what is expected of them before they begin work. Groups probably work best after an initial teacher-led introduction; the whole class is initiated into the activity until they become familiar with it. Then it can be split into groups which will go on working at the one activity. Later, other activities will be introduced in the same way, until finally a 'circus' of events has been introduced, with different groups operating on one of several tasks.

The make-up of groups will vary according to the nature of the task, but it is vital that they remain flexible, changing from ability groupings for short periods when the teacher has discovered a common need, to friendship groups for the planning of plays, tape-recordings and so on. The value of group organisation goes beyond its economy. The concept of 'sharing reading' is an important one which may change a child's whole attitude and motivation. From the age of seven upwards children are in a gregarious stage of social development. The idea of 'private, solitary reading' does not fit in with the self-image which many of them have; a realisation that other children are reading the same books but perhaps have a different opinion from their own about them helps children to decentre, and indeed helps them to think more critically about what they are reading.

The sharing of reading is emphasised by Don Holdaway, who calls it 'Shared-book-experience' (Holdaway op. cit.). He believes that every morning should start with a collecting-together of reading experiences from the previous day, when snippets will be read out by teacher and individuals, and when what has been read will be discussed briefly or summarised. Reading plans for the day will also be proposed. This means that children will be reading out passages that they have already prepared to a natural audience which has developed the habit of listening to each other. It also implies that reading may have been brought from home for sharing.

It has been suggested above that the success of group reading depends largely on the nature of the activities set. These may be of two basic kinds, the first aiming to give children practice in the development of reading skill, which will include a minimum of reading aloud, and a great deal of silent reading with discussion outcomes. Group cloze and group prediction would fall into this broad category. Group cloze entails a group discussing deletions in a passage with the aim of sharing opinions rather than reaching right answers. When the children have talked about possibilities they may be presented with the original text showing the author's choice of words. There is no need to make regular deletions, and in fact the value of group cloze depends very much on the careful choice of deletions.

Group prediction is similarly designed to encourage open-ended discussion. A story (or factual text with strong sequencing) is split into about four parts. Each child in the group reads the first part silently, and then the group discuss together what might happen next, basing their hypotheses on the passage they have read. The whole story is gradually distributed, until the presentation of the final episode. These techniques are described fully in Walker's *Reading Development and Extension* (1974).

The second kind of activity will aim to give children the opportunity to develop the skills of reading aloud for an audience. They will at first read to each other in the security of their small, probably self-chosen group, and will prepare in that group to read to the whole class, to other groups, or to other classes. Such activities could include the following:

1   Making individual anthologies of favourite poems and excerpts (copied with care). The group listen to each other's choices read aloud, and eventually select items for a programme to read to others. Anthologies should include choices from the children's own writing.

2   Learning poems by heart from their anthologies, for subsequent delivery (such learning, which of course involves reading and re-reading, being an almost forgotten activity in many classrooms!)

3   Reading out instructions to a partner in order that he can carry them out – making a model, following a recipe etc. These may be instructions from a book or game, or written by the child himself.

4   Group compiles a tape-recording of excerpts selected by them to illustrate a theme; for example, episodes from books which describe storms, people who are lost, children who are naughty, stories of changed identity etc. The themes should arise from the children's interests, but it will probably be necessary initially to provide a list of suggestions.

5   Group prepares for reading in assembly. Since 'performance' techniques will be needed in this case, discussion with the teacher will throw up different ways of delivering the material. For example, the ways in which the text can be divided with one child narrating and others taking individual parts.

6   Group reads from *Take Part* books, where dialogue is divided

according to different levels of readability. These books, published by Ward Lock Educational, adapt well-known stories in dialogue form, with the individual parts graded for readability. This ensures that the less skilled reader may be given an easy part, with the competent reader being suitably stretched.

7 Members of group bring books from home to read out favourite parts to each other. This will encourage sharing of books, summarising the stories, and so on.

8 Group plans and presents a radio advertisement, which can be tape-recorded for the class to hear.

9 Group brings a descriptive passage to life by reading it on tape with sound effects.

10 Group chooses a paragraph or even a sentence from a book which they are sharing, and tries out as many different ways as they can think of to read it aloud. They discuss which is the most effective. Why?

11 Reading stories to younger children. This will be preceded by choosing the stories (or even writing them), decisions about suitability, abridgement and so on.

12 Group adapts a story or poem for dramatisation.

Some books are better than others to read aloud, and children could help teachers to compile a list of 'sure-fire winners'. Ghost stories would probably win hands down, but there are many humorous interludes in books which are almost as satisfying.

CLASS TEACHING

Reading aloud in a class context has become almost entirely the prerogative of the teacher, owing to the deserved disrepute of 'reading round the class', which resulted in about a third of the class reading ahead and the same number becoming public failures in their attempts to decode difficult words. The rightfully important place given to the teacher reading stories ensures that children have a model of communicative reading and an introduction to stories that they can appreciate without necessarily being able to read them individually. There still seems to be a place, however, for occasional class instruction, rather than straight reading, and Don Holdaway suggests how the reading aloud session may also include direct teaching (Holdaway, 1979).

He pinpoints the difficulty of aligning individualised teaching with the reality of large classes, and puts forward the idea that corporate learning has always been a powerful mode (quoting initiation ceremonies, playground games and church services as examples). These models have non-competitiveness in common; 'they are entered into to be *like* other people. . . . Truly corporate activities are concerned with ego-sharing. . . . If we can achieve this corporate spirit, there is no reason why a large class cannot learn together' (pp. 64–5).

Reading aloud to children from a book held by the teacher does not allow for the sharing of what is on the page, and although she may show pictures from time to time, young children may not realise that it is *words* that are being read. Holdaway suggests that the use of enlarged texts with infants can help them to understand the conventions of print. From the teacher's selection of about twenty books to read to her class, three or four are picked out and rewritten in print large enough to be seen from the back of the class. It might be possible to enlist older children to copy the books neatly. Illustrations are supplied, as the story is read, by the children themselves. An overhead projector could be used equally well. The story, preferably containing repetition (for example, 'The Three Billy Goats Gruff'), is read by the teacher, while she runs a pointer along the lines of text. Gradually the children begin to join in the reading, especially in the parts they have heard before, and will begin to recognise the recurring visual patterns.

The children refer to the large books individually during the day, and sometimes take them home to share with their parents. Occasionally the teacher masks words with long strips of cardboard (particularly easy with an overhead projector), so that the masked parts can be predicted by the class. 'You can make a transparency with hinged words that can be flipped over into a slot at the right time – or even better, you can make several hinges exposing letter detail progressively' (Holdaway, 1979). A sliding masker allows for the highlighting of any word or letter in order to discuss it further:

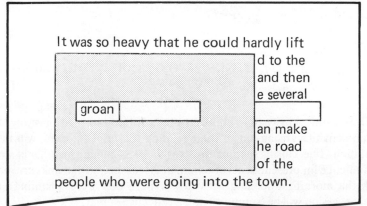

Holdaway thinks that books used in this way should be chosen for interest rather than readability level. He gives valuable suggestions for suitable texts, including *The very hungry caterpillar* (Carle, 1974), Dr Seuss books (published by Collins), *Where the wild things are* (Sendak, 1970) and *Bears in the night* (Berenstain and Berenstain, 1981). This method seems a promising way of developing word-recognition skills with a class while still preserving the context and enjoyment of the whole story. Although initially the production of the books would be time-consuming, a gradually built collection of enlarged books could form an attractive corner of the library.

Although this book has concentrated on ways of utilising reading aloud, it is of course only part of the total reading activity going on throughout the day. It may be useful, as Holdaway suggests, for a teacher to think of organisation in terms of reading processes and activities as well as the content of separate lessons. He gives a table which breaks down the organisation of a typical 'period', which may be of varying lengths:

Activity	Time	40 mins	60 mins	90 mins
Opening activities	5-10%	3-4	4-6	7-9
Quiet Time (Teacher conferences, Silent reading)	25-30%	10-12	15-18	25-30
Activity Time, including reading and study, conferences and group teaching	40-45%	15-18	25-30	35-40
Closing Session	10-15%	4-6	6-10	10-15

ACTUAL READING EXTENDS BEYOND 'QUIET TIME' MAKING UP ABOUT 40-50%

During the activity time children may continue to read or study, but group activities arising out of their reading (described above), will be in operation. The 'closing session' involves the class coming together again as an audience for presentations or to join in discussion, so that links are made with the morning's opening activities. Where they were 'planning', the closing session will be 'summing up', a reflective survey.

In this way the children have daily experience of the lively relevance of print to all the major human concerns which currently preoccupy them at their particular stage of development. Although only ten to fifteen per cent of the total period is spent in these terminal sharing sessions, it becomes a vital and satisfying part of the programme, giving the lie to that suspicion of personal isolation which hangs round the word 'individualised' (Holdaway, op. cit. p. 25).

Having discussed the organisation of record-keeping, and of time, in the classroom, we are left with the organisation of space and resources with regard to oral reading. Most infant classrooms have a reading corner, manoeuvred often through negotiation with parents and community, which invites entry with its carpet, bookshelves and cushions. Fewer such corners are found in junior classrooms, which seems a pity. If miscue analysis is to be carried out, there must be a quiet area where tape-recording can proceed, and if children are practising to read aloud for communication they equally require a peaceful spot. Many teachers make do with corridors, medical rooms and so on, but ideally the reading should happen where the books are, so that selection can be made easily and naturally.

A slight readjustment to book stocks would need to be considered if the activities suggested in early chapters are to work successfully. There will already be single copies of attractive stories available, but, in addition, small sets of half-a-dozen books of the same title will be needed for group reading. More information books which give instructions for carrying out simple processes (recipes, how-to-make-it manuals), would help in encouraging one child to read out instructions to his partner.

Tape-recorders are essential, and it is surprising that so few of the readily available cheap cassette recorders are not seen in use. Individual earphones are an admirable addition; somehow the exclusion of extraneous noise helps a child who is listening and following the text in the book to transfer to its private world. In some open plan classrooms they too are a necessity rather than a luxury.

SUMMING-UP

An attempt has been made in this book to analyse the ways in which oral reading may be used profitably in the classroom, with a view to the development of soundly-based, versatile reading strategies. The following ten points sum up the most important aspects which need to be borne in mind when planning reading activities.

1 Reading aloud is valuable, but its functions should be defined and differentiated: as a diagnostic instrument, as a means of instruction, and for communication to an audience.

2 When a child reads to the teacher he should be encouraged to see this as a problem-solving activity.

3 The child should be helped to use all cueing systems as soon as possible.

4 He should be introduced to the terms which describe reading, and encouraged to talk about the strategies he is using.

5 A main aim of hearing children read aloud is to encourage the early development of silent reading.

6 Children should read aloud to each other as well as to the teacher, and to share their opinions on specific books.

7 Merely working through a graded reading scheme will not ensure transfer from 'learning to read' to 'reading to learn'.

8 Talking about reading and the content of books is as valuable as hearing reading.

9 Comprehension may not tally with ease in reading aloud; a fluent oral reader may have poor recall, and a stumbling reader may understand what he has read.

10 Teacher and child should both participate in planning and evaluating an individual reading programme.

Reading remains a mysterious and complex process. The perceptual skills involved in word-recognition, and the internalisation of phrases which occur frequently in text, can only develop through practice, which may on occasion include rote-learning. Unless, though, the learner is able to slot his practised skills into an overall schema which is cognitively derived, he may never become a mature, efficient reader. However frequently a teacher hears a child read, only a sample of possible words and their combinations will be encountered. The aim of the reading interview should therefore be to help him towards independent mastery; practice is not its prime aim. Practice in reading can only be carried out by the child himself, and much time must be allotted for this. A variety of purposes devised to encourage functional reading, both oral and silent, will ensure that the 'practice' does not become mere rote repetition.

Much emphasis has been put upon miscue analysis, and this is only partly because of its direct diagnostic value. The importance of learning from children's mistakes is based on a theory which goes beyond reading, recognising that language learners set out to make rules for themselves, even if the rules themselves are faulty at first. Linguists have shown how early speech development is patterned in this way, and in an excellent book on writing development, Mina Shaughnessy (1979) draws similar conclusions. The final quotation is from her book, to remind us how close are the links between learning to talk, to read and to write:

I have reached the persuasion that underlies this book – namely, that students write the way they do, not because they are slow or non-verbal, indifferent to or incapable of academic excellence, but because they are beginners and must, like all beginners, learn by making mistakes. These they make aplenty and for such a variety of reasons that the inexperienced teacher is almost certain to see nothing but a chaos of error when he first encounters their papers. Yet a closer look will reveal very little that is random or 'illogical' in what they have written. And the keys to their development as writers often lie hidden in the very features of their writing that English teachers have been trained to brush aside. . . . The work must be informed by an understanding not only of what is missing or awry but of why it is so (p. 5).

Bibliography

ALTICK, R. D. (1975) 'The English Common Reader: A history of the mass reading public, 1800–1900' in LAWTON, D. (ed.) (1975) *Class, Culture and the Curriculum*. London: Routledge and Kegan Paul.

ATKINSON, E. and GAINS, C. (1979) *A New A–Z List of Reading Books*. N.A.R.E.

BASSEY, M. (1978) *Nine Thousand Primary School Teachers*. Slough: N.F.E.R.

BERENSTAIN, S. and BERENSTAIN, J. (1981) *Bears in the night*. Glasgow: Collins.

BERG, LEILA (ed.) *Nippers*. Basingstoke: Macmillan Education.

BETTS, A. and WELCH, C. (1964) *Informal Reading Inventories*. New York: American Book Co.

BIEMILLER, A. (1970) 'The development of the use of graphic and contextual information as children learn to read', *Reading Research Quarterly*, VI, 1.

BRICKETT, G. (1978) *Teachers' Reading Programmes*. Peterborough County Board of Education, Canada.

BULLOCK, SIR A. (ed.) (1975) *A Language for Life*. London: H.M.S.O.

BURT, SIR C., (1974 revision) *Burt Word Reading Test*. London: Hodder and Stoughton.

CAMPBELL, R. (1981) 'An approach to analysing teacher verbal moves in hearing children read', *Journal of Research in Reading*, U.K.R.A., 4, 1.

CARLE, E. (1974) *The very hungry caterpillar*. Harmondsworth: Penguin Books.

CASHDAN, A. (1969) 'Backward readers – research on auditory-visual integration' in Gardner, W. K. (ed.) *Reading skills: theory and practice*. London: Ward Lock Educational.

CHAPMAN, L. J. and CZERNIEWSKA, P. (1978) *Reading: from process to practice*. London: Routledge and Kegan Paul.

CHARLES, C. M. (1980) *Individualising Instruction*. Toronto: C. V. Mosby Co.

CHOMSKY, C. (1976) 'After Decoding: What?', *Language Arts*, 53, 3.

CLARK, M. (1976) *Young Fluent Readers*. London: Heinemann Educational.

CLAY, M. (1971) 'Juncture, Pitch and Stress as reading behaviour variables', *Journal of Verbal Behaviour and Verbal Learning*, 10 (pp. 133–9).

CLAY, M. (1972) *Reading: the Patterning of Complex Behaviour*. London: Heinemann Educational.

DONALD, D. R. (1980) 'Analysis of children's reading errors, a current perspective', *Journal of Research in Reading*, 3, 2.

GIBSON, E. J. and LEVIN, H. (1975) *The Psychology of Reading*. Cambridge, Mass. and London: M.I.T. Press.

GIGLIOLI, P. (ed.) (1972) *Language and Social Context*. Harmondsworth: Penguin Education.

GOODACRE, E. (1977) *Reading after Ten*. London: BBC.

GOODACRE, E. (1979 New edn) *Hearing Children Read*. Reading Centre, Reading University.

GOODMAN, K. (1968) 'Reading: a psycholinguistic guessing game', *Journal of the Reading Specialist*, 6, pp. 126–35.

GOODMAN, K. (1969) 'Analysis of oral reading miscues: applied psycholinguistics', *Reading Research Quarterly*, 1, 3.

GOODMAN, Y. and BURKE, C. (1972) *Reading Miscue Inventory*. New York: Macmillan.

GOODY, J. and WATT, I. (1972) 'The Consequences of Literacy' in GIGLIOLI, P. (ed.) (1972) *Language and Social Context*. Harmondsworth: Penguin Education.

GULLIVER, J. (1979) 'Teachers' Assumptions in Listening to Reading' in *Language for Learning*, University of Exeter, 1.

H.M.S.O. (1944) *A Handbook of Suggestions for Teachers*.

H.M.S.O. (1959) *Primary Education*.

H.M.S.O. (1978) *Primary Education in England*, a survey by H.M. Inspectors of Schools.

HOLDAWAY, D. (1972) *Independence in Reading*. Auckland, New Zealand: Ashton Scholastic.

HOLDAWAY, D. (1979) *The Foundations of Literacy*. Auckland, New Zealand: Ashton Scholastic.

HUEY, E. B. (1908) *The Psychology and Pedagogy of Reading*. New York: Macmillan.

HUGHES, J. (1975) *Reading and Reading Failure*. London: Evans Bros.

HUNTER-GRUNDIN, E. (1979) *Literacy, a systematic start*. New York: Harper and Row.

JOHNSON, M. and KRESS, R. (1965) *Informal Reading Inventories*. Newark, Delaware: I.R.A.

KAVANAGH, J. F. and MATTINGLY, I. G. (eds) (1979) *Language by Ear and Eye – the relationship between speech and writing*. Cambridge, Mass. and London: M.I.T. Press.

LANE, S. and KEMP, M. (eds) (1976) *Take Part* series. London: Ward Lock Educational.

LAWTON, D. (ed.) (1975) *Class, Culture and the Curriculum*. London: Routledge and Kegan Paul.

LUNZER, E. and GARDNER, K. (1979) *The Effective Use of Reading*. London: Heinemann Educational for the Schools Council.

MCCRACKEN, R. A. (ed.) (1964) 'Improvement of Reading through Classroom Practice', *I.R.A. Proceedings*, **9**.

MCGROGAN, S. (1980) *Read, Think, Discuss*. Queen's University Belfast, Teachers' Centre.

MACKAY, D. *et al.* (1970) *Breakthrough to Literacy, Teachers' Manual*. London: Longman.

MCLUHAN, M. (1967) *The Gutenberg Galaxy*. London: Routledge and Kegan Paul.

MAXWELL, J. (1977) *Reading Progress from 8 to 15*. Slough: N.F.E.R. Publishing Co.

MINISTRY OF EDUCATION (1950) *Reading Ability: some suggestions for helping the backward*, Pamphlet 18. London: H.M.S.O.

MORRIS, R. (1979 new edn) *Success and Failure in Learning to Read*. Harmondsworth: Penguin Books.

MOYLE, D. (1968) *The Teaching of Reading*. London: Ward Lock Educational.

NEALE, M. (1958) *The Analysis of Reading Ability*. London: Macmillan.

PLOWDEN, LADY, (ed.) (1967) *Children and their Primary Schools*, Vol. 1. London: H.M.S.O.

PUGH, A. K. (1978) *Silent Reading: an introduction to its study and teaching*. London: Heinemann Educational.

PUMFREY, P. (1976) *Reading: Tests and Assessment Techniques*. London: Hodder and Stoughton for U.K.R.A.

PUMFREY, P. (1977) *Measuring Reading Abilities*. London: Hodder and Stoughton.

RAGGETT, M., TUTT, C. and RAGGETT, P. (1979) *Assessment and Testing of Reading: Problems and Practices*. London: Ward Lock Educational.

READING 360 (1978) The Ginn Reading Programme. Aylesbury: Ginn.

REED, D. (1970) 'Linguistic Forms and the Process of Reading' in LEVIN and WILLIAMS (eds) *Basic Studies on Reading*. New York and London: Basic Books Inc.

REID, J. F. (1958) 'An Investigation of Thirteen Beginners in Reading', *Acta Psychologica*, **14**, 4, pp. 295–313.

REID, J. F. (1966) 'Learning to think about reading', *Educational Research*, **9**, pp. 56–62.

REID, J. F. (1973) *The Link-up Programme*. Aberdeen: Holmes-McDougall.

ROTHKOPF, E. Z. (1972) in CARROLL, J. and FREEDLE, R. (eds) *Language, Comprehension and the Acquisition of Knowledge*. New York: Winston/ Wiley.

SARTRE, J-P. (1967) *Words*. Harmondsworth: Penguin Books.

SCHONELL, F. J. (1945) *The Psychology and Teaching of Reading*. London: Oliver and Boyd.

SCHONELL, F. J. and SCHONELL, F. E. (1945) *Graded Word Reading Test.* London: Oliver and Boyd.

SCHONELL, F. J. and SERJEANT, L. (1939) *Happy Venture Readers.* Edinburgh: Oliver and Boyd.

SENDAK, M. (1970) *Where the wild things are.* Harmondsworth: Penguin Books.

SEUSS, DR, Dr Seuss Books. Glasgow: Collins.

SHAUGNESSY, M. P. (1979) *Errors and Expectations*. New York: Oxford University Press.

SINCLAIR, J. and COULTHARD, R. (1975) *Towards an analysis of discourse.* Oxford: Oxford University Press.

SMITH, F. (1973) *Psycholinguistics and Reading*. New York: Holt, Rinehart & Winston.

SMITH, F. (1978) (second edn) *Understanding Reading*. New York: Holt, Rinehart & Winston.

SOUTHGATE, BOOTH, V., ARNOLD, H. and JOHNSON, S. (1981) *Extending Beginning Reading*. London: Heinemann Educational for the Schools Council.

SPACHE, G. (1953) 'A new Readability formula for Primary Grade reading materials', *Elementary School Journal*, **53**, March.

START, K. B. and WELLS, B. K. (1972) *The Trend of Reading Standards*. Slough: N.F.E.R.

WALKER, C. (1974) *Reading Development and Extension*. London: Ward Lock Educational.

WEAVER, C. (1980) *Psycholinguistics and Reading: from process to practice*. Cambridge, Mass.: Winthrop Publishers, Inc.

Index